COPS' TRUE STORIES OF THE PARANORMAL

GHOSTS, UFOS, AND OTHER SHIVERS

LOREN W. CHRISTENSEN

Copyright © 2016 Loren W. Christensen
Revised 2018

No part of this book may be reproduced in any form
without written permission from the author.
All rights reserved

To those men and women who don't call 911
They are 911

Contents

Introduction 1
Terminology 7

Section One: On Patrol 19
    Vanished 25
    Trapped 28
    Eyes 32
    Dead Man Walking 38
    Dead Man's Cane 40
    A Touch Of Thanks 42
    The Snitch 45
    The Couple 50
    The Warning 53
    The Light 57
    Wrong Number 60
    On Patrol In The News 62

Section Two: Haunted Places 69
    Jails And Prisons 71
    Ghost Prisoner 73
    Tower 7 75
    The Eternally Caring Nurse 79
    Some Stayed Behind 82
    The Drawing T-Minus 1 Hour, 46 Minutes 85

Hospitals 88
Nurse Betty, The "Haint" 89
Hospital Morgue 93
Other Haunted Places 96
Coffee And Cups 99
The Stabber 104
The Faceless Mannequin 109
White Eagle 113
The Man In The Window 116
Strange Place 119
Forest Lawn Cemetery 124
Haunted Places In The News 128

Section Three: Divine Intervenion And Demons 137
Scratches 141
A Sign In Twisted Metal 144
The Voice 146
He Pulled The Trigger Four Times 152
Divine Intervention In The News 158

Section Four: UFOs 163
Close Encounters Of The Second Kind 167
UFOs And Cow Mutilations In The News 178

Conclusion 187
About The Author 189
Other Books By Loren W. Christensen 191

ACKNOWLEDGEMENTS

A big hug to my wonderful wife, Lisa, for her encouragement and for taking the photos sprinkled throughout this book.

A manly hug to my friend Kevin Faulk for eyeballing the manuscript for typos and other errors.

A huge thanks to the men and women who contributed their experiences to this text. Stay safe out there.

At first cock-crow
The ghosts must go
Back to their quiet graves below
~Theodosia Garrison, "The Neighbors"

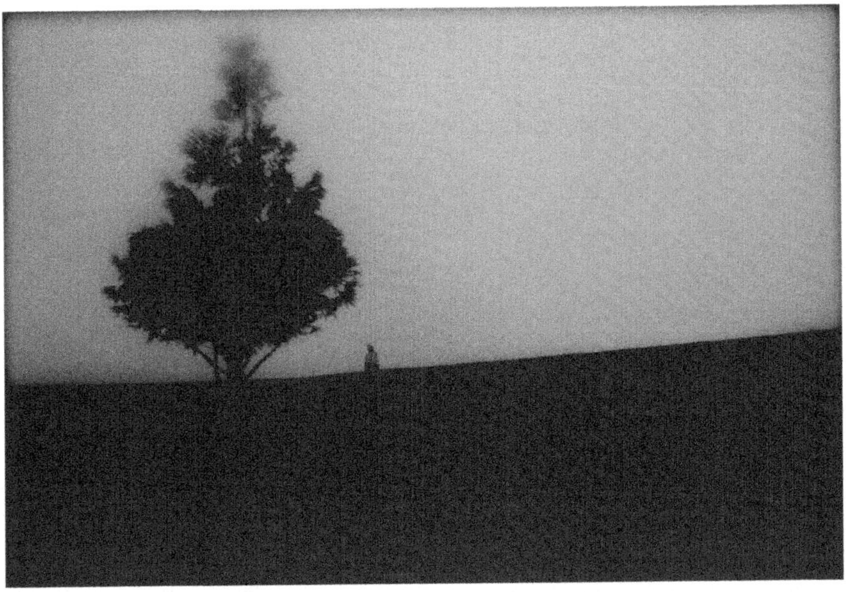

INTRODUCTION

Cops, corrections officers, military police, and security people see life differently than those outside of law enforcement. Depending on the job and location, some see more madness, tragedy, bloody violence, and man's inhumanity to man in a month than most people experience in a lifetime. People on the job have been there, done that, seen it all, heard it all, and experienced it all.

Because people lie to the police every day, people in law enforcement have a fine-tuned b.s. detector. Even rookies quickly understand the two primary rules in law enforcement.

Rule 1: Everyone lies.
Rule 2: See Rule 1.

"I don't trust people; they tend to lie. Evidence never lies." Gil Grissom, *CSI*.

Law enforcement people trust the evidence. Experienced officers know how crooks think and they know how bad guys operate when committing certain crimes. They recognize the pattern of street drug sales, residential burglaries, armed robberies, sexual assaults, gang graffiti, mass shootings, and so on. Yes, there are variations in all of these areas, but there are certain basics that help officers know immediately, or soon after, the nature of the situation.

That said, ever so often something happens that doesn't fall neatly into a category in which cops typically function, nor does it fall into any of the unusual situations that occur from time to time in law enforcement. No, these are events that go beyond the unusual. These are aberrations, oddities, and the eerie that do not fit in any logical box.

As a result, it confuses, it causes anxiety, stress, and often leaves the officer feeling alone. To tell others about the aberration is to invite teasing, ridicule, and an even greater sense of feeling isolated from peers. People in law enforcement are no different than the general population in that they have their doubters, disbelievers, and scorners. That is until something happens to the disbelievers. As paranormal investigator, Jim Pace of Sooner Paranormal of Oklahoma says, "I love to take skeptics along [on an investigation]. The difference between a believer and a skeptic is personal experience."

The men and women who tell their stories in this book did so for whatever personal reasons they had. Although I never asked, I got the impression from some that they were happy to have an outlet—no doubt after living in silence for so long—where they could tell their strange tale(s).

I have included incidents that happened to me. In one story, titled "Close Encounters of the Second Kind," I write about how dozens of Army missile specialists, and my military police buddies and I worked around UFOs for several weeks. While I've told friends and family about it over the decades, I've never before written about it. Will I get ridiculed? Probably. But I felt sharing it was more important than worrying about what others think, especially those who haven't experience anything.

Perhaps that is why some of the other writers came forward.

My role in this book

I'm not an investigator of the paranormal and supernatural. I consider myself an interested party, a reporter. I have had experiences as I relate in these pages, but I wasn't investigating such things when they happened. I was simply going through the motions of my job when caught flatfooted.

Such was the case with other cops, deputies, MPs, security officers, and correction officers who tell their stories within.

My minor "investigative" experience

I did have a brief investigative foray into things that go bump in the night, but not as a cop.

A few years ago, my agent talked to me about writing a book on the long-running TV program, *Ghost Hunters*. The deal eventually went away, but not before my wife and I read a ton of books, watched DVDs, videos, attended a meeting with ghost hunters, and made a few excursions—armed with digital cameras and an audio recording device—into cemeteries, mausoleums, and old houses.

When reporters asked notorious bank robber Willie Sutton why he continued robbing banks after the police had caught him so many times, he answered with a shrug, "Because that's where the money is." So, we thought we would begin our investigation in the most logical places: cemeteries and mausoleums because, well, that's where the dead people are. The argument against this idea is that spirits don't hang out around their burial site; they seek out their loved ones or remain in places they enjoyed. My wife and I knew this theory, but we wanted to start out slowly and get some experience at using our limited equipment.

We began in a mausoleum so massive it had its own weather pattern. Maybe not, but it seemed like it, anyway. It was a sprawling complex built on the side of a large hill, with three stories above ground and three or four below. There were thousands of deceased inside, most of them resting in marble covered drawers and the others in glass-encased urns. The place was dead quiet, to use an obvious descriptor, except for a mysterious sound of water trickling from somewhere and the occasional echoing footsteps of visitors, living, and perhaps, otherwise.

We spent an afternoon walking about snapping pics in hopes of capturing orbs, and sitting for long periods with a listening device while asking the room questions like, "Is there anyone here that would like to talk with us?" We didn't capture an image of an orb, nor did we get an EVP, electronic voice phenomenon (see "Terminology" page). We even enhanced our recordings on a laptop.

The mausoleum had an incredibly thick atmosphere with a profound silence that reminded us how loud was our respective tinnitus. There was something immediately compelling about the place, as well as off-putting. Before we knew it, we had spent three hours inside, though we had only explored a fraction of the place.

So we went back the next week.

This time we stayed for about 90 minutes. We didn't have a set time for the visit, and we might have stayed longer, but we both suddenly began feeling awful. My wife became profoundly fatigued, so much so she just wanted to sleep on one of the marble benches. I abruptly grew angry, exceptionally so. All the way home, I thought about pulling motorists out of cars and beating them into a paste. Our intense feelings came on simultaneously and for no apparent reason.

The trip from the mausoleum to our house took about 40 minutes. After pulling into the driveway, we remained in the car, both of us too drained to get out. Also, we wondered if it was a good idea to go into the house carrying with us whatever we had brought home. So we sat in the driveway. We had a function to go to that night, but we gave serious thought to canceling, though the tickets were expensive.

Happily, we slowly began to recover from whatever had hitched onto us. My wife's energy returned and so did my usual happy-go-lucky self, though we still felt a tad out of sorts. We eventually got out of the car and went to the symphony, but we agreed we would not return to the stadium-sized mausoleum—ever.

We also took three ghost tours: Victoria, Canada, San Francisco, and the Queen Mary in Long Beach, California. They were all fun and atmospheric, but only the Queen Mary gave us experiences. When we entered the ship's long-empty swimming pool area, my wife's movie camera immediately ceased to work. We were told the extremely haunted area regularly sucked the life out of visitors' electronic instruments. Rattling us even more was that the camera began working again the moment we left the area.

We also felt a dramatic temperature change in two different places. The tour guide called them a vortex, an opening to the other side. Whatever they were, they were small enough to move our hands through and feel a difference.

Sometime after our negative experience at the large mausoleum we decided to give another one a try. It was a smaller building, one level, and L-shaped. It was a typical mausoleum, mostly gray marble, cool, and with sporadic flowers sticking out from wall mounts. And silence. There's quiet, and then there's mausoleum quiet.

I didn't bring the EVP recorder, but Lisa had the digital and was strolling about snapping pics in hopes of capturing an elusive orb. She took dozens without success—except for one photo.

We separated at one point; she was around the corner in one leg of the L and I, having lost interest in spirit hunting, was reading the names and dates on the many drawers. At one point, I sat down on a bench lost in thought; the only sound my wife's camera clicking away in the distance.

Suddenly I felt quite cold. The temperature seemed to have instantaneously dropped 10 or 15 degrees. I looked all around for an air vent, but I didn't find one, or any other source of the drop in temperature. Besides, it didn't feel like the cold produced by a fan or an air conditioner. It felt, I don't know. Different.

I could hear my wife's camera clicks growing louder as she approached the corner from the other long hall. I sat motionless, almost afraid to move. I kept watching the corner waiting for her to round it. Finally, there she was, snapping merrily at anything and everything.

"What?" she whispered, apparently seeing the look on my face.

"Take. My. Picture." I said, sans lip movement like a ventriloquist, so as not to disturb ... I didn't know what.

"Cold spot," I managed.

She quickly raised the digital and snapped one photo. It would be the only picture out of all the ones she took that day, and the other two days at the big mausoleum, to depict a large orb—hovering by my chest.

A few minutes later, the cold pocket was no longer.

TERMINOLOGY

Here is a list of terms applicable to the stories found in this book. As is often the case in specialty fields, experts and students don't always agree as to definitions in the paranormal and supernatural world. In fact, there is often disagreement on how to interpret observations and findings. (Sounds like law enforcement, doesn't it?) Therefore, the following definitions are a composite from many sources.

First, the agencies represented in this text.

LAW ENFORCEMENT

Campus Police
Campus police or university police are employed by a college or university to protect the campus and surrounding areas, and the people who live, work and visit it.

Urban Police Officer
Men and woman that maintain regular patrols and respond to calls for service in cities, large and small. Patrol officers are assigned to patrol specific areas, such as parks, neighborhoods, and within the city. They routinely work in cars, on horses, bicycles, and on foot patrol.

Sheriff and Deputy Sheriff

Men and women who enforce laws at the county level. A sheriff, who is elected, performs duties like those of a city police chief. A deputy sheriff in a large agency has duties similar to officers in urban police departments.

Detective

A detective, no matter what police agency, gathers facts and collects evidence for criminal cases. They conduct interviews, examine records, observe the activities of suspects, and participate in raids and arrests.

State Police

Also known as highway patrol officers, these men and women arrest criminals statewide and patrol highways to enforce motor vehicle laws and regulations. They direct traffic at the scene of accidents, provide first aid, and call for emergency equipment.

Military Police

MPs are law enforcement officers serving in the military. They protect the lives and property on Army installations by enforcing military laws and regulations. They also control traffic, prevent crime, and respond to all emergencies.

Security Officer

A security officer (guard) is a civilian hired privately to protect property, assets, and people. They usually wear a uniform and serve to maintain a high-visibility to deter illegal and inappropriate actions.

Corrections Officer

A corrections officer is responsible for the care, incarceration, and control of people arrested and awaiting trial, or people convicted of a crime and sentenced to serve time in a prison or jail. They are also responsible for the safety and security of the facility itself. Usually, the government of the jurisdiction in which they operate hire officers, though private companies employ people, as well.

PARANORMAL TERMS

3:00 a.m.

A few paranormal investigators believe that activity increases around this time (some of the stories in this book occurred at 3 a.m., but most didn't). Some say that because Jesus died at 3:00 p.m., the demons come out at 3:00 a.m., the direct opposite. Those in opposition ask how this could be valid since no one knows the exact year Jesus died, let alone the precise time. Some long-time investigators get testy whenever the question arises because they say it's a concept that came from Washington Irving's book *Sleepy Hollow*, and therefore ridiculous.

Apparitions

An apparition is a full-body sighting of a ghost or spirit that wants the living to see them. Most sightings are partial or in the form of a mist or shadow and have a connection to a place or object. Many wear the same clothing and do the same things as when they lived. Some observers report the apparitions as good while other witnesses find them evil in some way.

Automatic Writing

Automatic writing is believed to be the process of unconsciously writing words or drawing pictures. The act doesn't come from the author's mind; it appears on paper without conscious awareness. Psychologists argue that it comes from the subconscious, while others believe it comes from the spirit world.

Cold Spot

A cold spot is a small space that is at least 10 degrees colder than the area surrounding it. The dropped temperature—paranormal investigators use instruments to measure the change—sometimes occurs suddenly and cannot be explained by the obvious: open windows or doors, air conditioning, or exposure to snow or ice. The phenomenon usually occurs in conjunction with sightings, moved objects, and sounds.

Divine Intervention

Divine intervention is a direct and obvious intervention in the affairs of humans by a deity.

Ghost

A ghost is the residual energy of a person or animal. It's believed not to be an intelligent form but rather a kind of "recording," that is, an image or sound similar to an audio or video that continuously replays. Sometimes the energy weakens over time, but other times it somehow recharges.

Ghost Lights

These are an outdoor phenomenon, usually seen from a distance. Most often, witnesses report balls of light, sometimes rod-shaped, that move at varying speeds. Typically, they are white, but they can also be yellow, orange, red, blue, and green. Some observers say the lights are swamp gas or reflections of car lights. Others think they are UFOs (which technically is true), while a few eyewitnesses believe they are ghosts or spirits.

Hauntings

We often think of a haunting as a full-body apparition, but those are considered quite rare. Typically, a haunting involves noises—footsteps, music, sounds, or voices—that occur any time of the day. Sometimes they last for only a few days while other times they go on for years. Hauntings might arise on specific dates, a special anniversary, or the same time each day. They can happen on an eerie foggy night or a bright sunny day.

Hauntings can be seen, heard, smelled, and touched. Witnesses often feel unexplained cold or hot spots in a location, as well as breezes. Some people report an odor of flowers, cigarette smoke, or perfume associated with a deceased loved one. The association might be unknown.

Hauntings can affect your emotions. Some witnesses report a sense of dread, depression, irritation, and anger. Others experience the opposite. One person said she felt "cheery."

Intelligent Hauntings

Spirits interacting with the living are called intelligent hauntings. It's said they retain the same personality they had when alive, meaning kind people become kind spirits, and unpleasant people turn into troublesome spirits.

Knowing
Knowing that something is about to happen can also be called psychic, ESP (extra-sensory perception), and possessing a sixth sense.

Mutilation
For many decades, there have been reports of farmers and ranchers finding mutilated animals on their land. In most instances, the animals were missing eyes, sex organs, and other parts. This was almost always done with precision and without leaving blood. In some cases, evidence indicates the animal fell from a great height. (See the back of this book for information about my short story fiction titled *Parts*, which focuses on this phenomenon.)

Orb
Orbs are usually circular, sometimes visible to the naked eye but more commonly captured in photos. They move about seemingly at random and can quickly change direction. They appear both indoors and outside, sometimes twinkling and sometimes containing a nucleus or concentric circles. They often react in some fashion when people are near. The best orbs are those captured in photos when there are other phenomena present, such as apparitions, moving objects, and sounds.

False orbs—dust, raindrops, lights, insects, and snow—can be transparent, pale white, or blue.

Remote Viewing
One trained in remote viewing can perceive a target located in a nearby room, on the other side of the country, or anywhere in the world. To a skilled person, time and space are irrelevant. Remote viewing is different than ESP in that it uses specific techniques to conjure results.

Residual Haunting

Mentioned under the definition of "ghost," a residual haunting is the most common type of paranormal activity. Experienced investigators believe it's a result of trapped energy from a past event. For example, at the turn of last century, many witnesses reported the sounds of cannon fire, shouting men, and screaming horses at the Gettysburg battle site where over 50,000 men were killed or injured in three days.

Residual hauntings include sights, sounds, and smells. The ghost isn't aware of the living around them and thus unable to communicate. Therefore, the living can't convince the ghost to move on. It must dissipate over time, which could take years.

Sensitive

Commonly called an HSP, a highly sensitive person typical demonstrates these traits.

- A person who responds to occult influences.
- More caring and easily affected by the emotions of others.
- HSPs are more conscious of stimuli than others, such as noise, energy, light, atmosphere, odors, texture, and temperature.
- They are often in tune with the feelings and emotions of a spirit, and they can feel subtle nuances in paranormal events.
- Because of their ability in matters paranormal, an HSP can be religious or spiritual.
- They might view themselves as different from others because of their abilities.
- They are often thorough and exhaustive in their work, outside interests, and all other areas of their life.

- HSPs are most productive in a space that allows them to work quietly and without interruption.
- They are creative people who intensely enjoy art, music, and the beauty of the outdoors.
- They are not comfortable in an environment that is unclean or in disorder.
- Most HSP's are introverted and enjoy quiet time to replenish themselves.

~Thanks to Manchester Paranormal Investigations

Shadow People or Shadow Beings

Shadow people often appear in the corner of the eye. However, as we see in Colleen Formanek's story "Hospital Morgue" and in one of the news pieces, witnesses also see them in full body. Skeptics say it's nothing more than one's imagination, a trick of the eyes.

People who have experienced them say otherwise. Witnesses often say there is a sense of evil associated with the sightings, which has led some paranormal followers to wonder if they are demonic.

Spirit Possession

This occurs when a spirit temporarily or permanently attaches itself to a living person. Paranormal investigators refer to "partial possession" as when the attachment affects the victim's behavior to a limited extent, as opposed to completely taking them over, as seen in the movie, *The Exorcist*.

Spirit

A spirit is the soul of a person or animal that remains in this world after the body dies. Some paranormal investigators believe spirits have been to the afterlife but then return to revisit the living for some reason. They use sounds and smells to remind the living who they are.

Trapped Spirit

Fictional TV shows like *Ghost Whisperer* often depict a plotline in which a spirit is unable or reluctant to move on from this world to the next. But paranormal investigators say this is rare. When it does happen, it's called an "intelligent haunting" or "intelligent spirit" because the deceased is aware of where it is and of people, both of which are familiar to it. In some cases, however, experts believe a spirit was not connected to a place at all, but decided to dwell in it.

A trapped spirit might be confused and not know it's dead. They move on once they are made aware of their passing.

The spirit might want to say goodbye to a loved one and will appear to the living in dreams or when fully conscious. The spirit appears briefly and then moves on.

A spirit might have unfinished business and will stay as long as it takes to draw the attention of the living or until the business is completed.

There are many other reasons.

UFO

The unidentified flying object flies, but it can't be identified as an airplane, helicopter, weather balloon, bird, kite, or anything else that moves about the skies. Commonly, people associate UFOs with visitations by aircraft from another planet.

The lack of scientific study has given rise to researchers and groups outside of the scientific community, such as the Mutual UFO Network (MUFON) and the Center for UFO Studies (CUFOS). The word "Ufology" (you-fall-ogy) is used to describe the study of reports and related evidence of UFOs.

Vortex

A vortex can occur anywhere but most often is found in a home or building, or as noted in the Introduction, a ship. As usual, there isn't a consensus as to what it is. Some paranormal investigators say it's the spirit of the former resident of a home. Others believe it's a conduit to transport spirits—often in the shape of orbs—from the realm of the dead to the realm of the living. Still, others say it's a temporary opening to the other side.

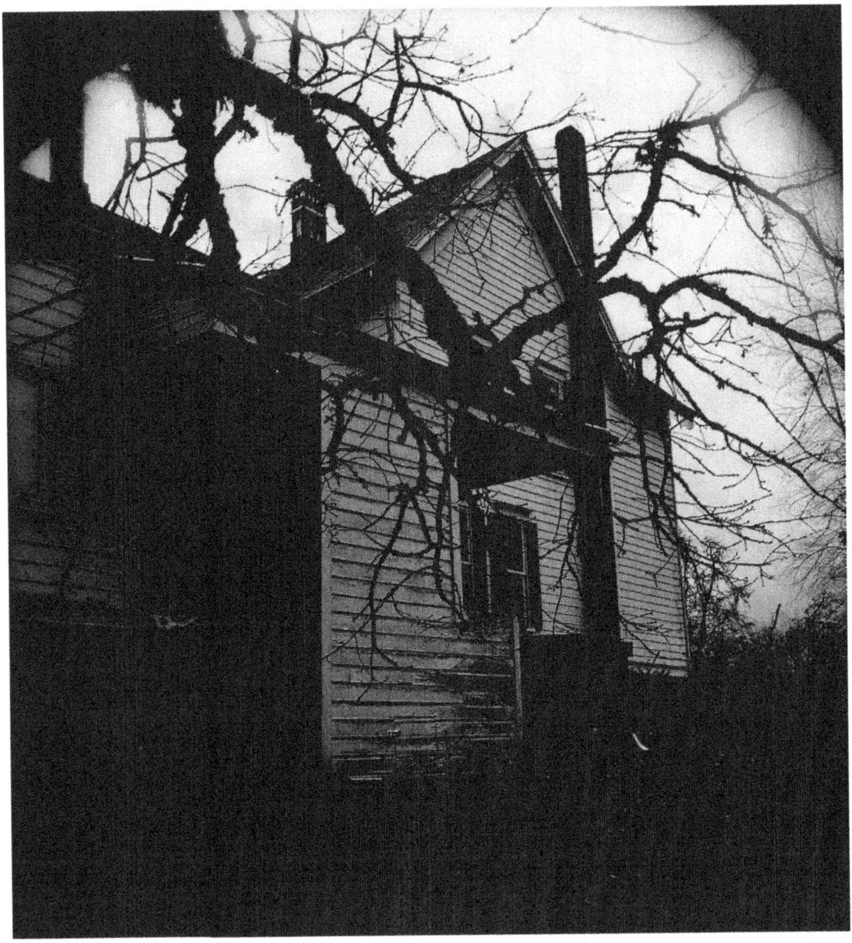

SECTION ONE

ON PATROL

My first night on patrol with my training coach turned into a long one. Instead of getting off at 11:45, we didn't return to the precinct until 4 a.m. A drunk driver had sailed off the road and into a slough, and we had to wait for a tow truck to extract it so we could get a body count.

My second night on the job, I stepped on an aorta, which 30 minutes earlier had been inside of a drunken stepfather's chest. But his 16-year-old stepson, angry from watching the man once again beat his mother with a glass ashtray, had retrieved a 12-guage shotgun loaded with slugs and fired one into the man's heart, blowing the aorta 10 feet down a hallway.

I was assigned the most active district in the city right out of the academy. As a recently returned Vietnam veteran, violence and gore didn't bother me as it did some non-vet rookies, but I was forced to learn the ways of a street cop at an accelerated rate. Within a few months, prowler calls, burglaries, drunk drivers, family fights, and bar brawls became routine, occasionally punctuated with a felony car stop at gunpoint, a man with a knife call, a terrible traffic accident, and a child abduction.

My experiences were probably no different than most cops that work in the city. Some would agree with me that although police calls involve different participants, at various locations, and under different circumstances, there is still a sameness to them. The complainants are similar, the suspects are the usual bottom feeders, and the paperwork is always the same. In time, street patrol becomes monotonous, routine. So how can a bar fight or a drunken car crash be mundane? When the officer has seen it all before a hundred, maybe hundreds of times.

Then on one occasion the officer sees *something*, hears *something*, or feels *something*, and it doesn't compute. It doesn't fit the norm of the police job (and the police norm is crazy, to begin with). In fact, it doesn't fit anything outside of it either. It isn't logical. It isn't normal. It doesn't fit the officer's self-prescribed rules, tactics, or worldview of how things are supposed to work.

The *something* I'm referring to is what this book is about: ghosts, spirits, UFOs, demons, ominous sounds, odd feelings, strange touches, sudden and profound depression, people vanishing in clear view, and haunted places.

In an article in the *Scientific American* ("Ghost Stories: Visits from the Deceased" December 2, 2008), the University of Goteborg found that over 80 percent of elderly people experienced hallucinations of their partner within a month after their passing. Almost one-third of the 80 percent reported that they had communicated with their partner.

On a personal note, a week or so after my mother died I was in my office working. As clear as a rung bell, I heard "Loren" whispered in her voice from behind me. I startled and turned around to find only an empty room. It was at once unnerving and comforting. Some would say she was saying goodbye.

The *Scientific American*, being scientific and all, call these sightings hallucinations. But they admit their knowledge ends there. They say, "Despite the fact that hallucinations are one of the most common reactions to loss, they have barely been investigated and we know little more about them." They then went on to say that most people reading the article will "re-experience the dead."

There are many, many stories in books, magazines, YouTube, and in blogs about the recently deceased being seen again by loved ones. There are also stories of people minutes away from death seeing loved ones who have already died waiting for them on the other side.

Cops respond to death scenes all the time. I patrolled an area for a while where I was getting at least one dead body call a week, so many that other officers were calling me the "Death Car." I didn't experience anything out of the ordinary at these, but other cops have, and unlike those in the *Scientific American* study, they didn't know the recently deceased.

Still, they experienced *something*.

VANISHED
By Kerry L. Wood

Roanoke's busy city center is abundant with striking historic buildings, fine dining, and a variety of small shops and large department stores where one can while away a fun-filled day. It's a medium-sized town with crime problems typical of other like-sized cities across the country. I served on the Roanoke Police Department for 27 years, retiring in 2002 as a detective sergeant.

In the mid-1980s, my partner, David Ragland, and I were working a burglary detail patrolling in uniform in an unmarked van. It was just before twilight when we spotted a suspicious looking vehicle moving slowly through a neighborhood. We began to tail him, thinking he was possibly casing houses, but he quickly made us and took off at a high rate of speed.

We called for a uniformed car to stop him and though he was doing 70 mph, we did our best to keep him in our sights as we followed in our unmarked. It eventually became apparent that he was heading toward Shaffer's Crossing, a 100-foot-long concrete railroad tunnel.

Pursuits are always risky and never more so than when a desperate man is pushing his vehicle close to 75 mph. Then, as quickly as it began, the pursuit came to an abrupt, explosive stop.

We'll never know if the driver overcompensated his steering, or lost control in a moment of panic, exhilaration, or any number of other causes. But for whatever reason, he navigated his two tons of steel, chrome, and rubber straight into the concrete archway.

Dave Ragland and I were about 200 feet behind the speeding car when it crashed, and we both watched in shock as the destroyed vehicle lifted about two feet into the air. We remained in control of our van and stopped behind the crash.

Just as shocking was when the suspect driver—a white male, 5 feet 10 inches, and husky at about 180 pounds—squeezed out of the small driver's window, seemingly unscathed, and dashed off into the tunnel.

As long-time partners are disposed to do, we didn't waste a second talking about it but instead took off at a dead run after the man. He was running hard but so were we, and we never lost sight of him. We managed to close the distance and got close enough to see him clearly. That is, until he—

—vanished.

We stopped. What the …?

There were no exits in the tunnel, period. We looked all around, examined every inch of the passageway, but there was simply no trace of him. None.

We were disconcerted, confused, and feeling every other kind of emotion as we reluctantly headed back to the tunnel's entrance. As we neared the crash site, we could see our van and the totaled suspect car, and—the driver.

The suspect.

It was the same man, clothes, height, and weight, we had just been chasing, but he was now sitting in the car, in the driver's seat. The steering wheel and the dashboard had crushed his chest, killing him.

Shocked, we managed to call for a supervisor and a traffic unit to come to the scene. We told him what had occurred: How we had spotted the suspicious vehicle, pursued it, witnessed the crash, ran after the driver, but lost him when he merely vanished right in front of us, only to find him a few minutes later behind the wheel of his car, his life crushed out.

The supervisor was an older and wiser man, especially in the ways of the department and how other cops think. He told us to write our reports but leave out all references to us pursuing the dead man on foot. In short, don't say anything about chasing the … spirit, or whatever it was.

***

David Ragland and I are both retired now and still friends. He is a very religious and church-going man and, while we have occasionally talked about that evening, he still has no opinion on what we saw. Nor do I. Both of us have discussed it with his minster, but no explanation has come forth from him either.

That is, no explanation other than we saw and chased the real spirit of the deceased driver still fleeing from the police.

TRAPPED

By Jess Burlingham

Dispatch said, "You got one not seen for several days, and the complainant says there's a foul odor coming from his apartment."

"One not seen" is never a good call, especially on a steamy 95-degree July day with the humidity dense enough to support aquatic life. Whenever I had one of these, it was always such a pleasure to step outside afterward and take a deep breath, not only to cleanse my lungs but also to exhale the image of death from my head before going on to the next call. But this time it was different.

This time something left with me.

The awful stench was apparent from the parking lot, though the location in question was 303, three floors up, and it only got worse as we climbed the stairs. The complainant lived two apartments away and told us she hadn't seen Mr. Jones, who was in his late 40s, for a week. When she smelled the terrible odor, she decided it was time to call the police.

The complex's maintenance man met us in front of the apartment, unlocked the door, and quickly left, leaving us to open it, either for legal reasons or because he didn't want to get knocked back by the smell. Smart guy.

We opened it a crack and announced ourselves. "Richmond Police! Anybody home?"

Silence.

We nudged the door open to a blast of heat and an unbearably thick, gut-wrenching odor. I attempted to step inside, but the stench was so overpowering I had to back out. My partner gave it a try too, but he didn't make it any farther than I did. A third officer joined us, and he was also forced back out into the hallway. There was no doubt in our minds that Mr. Jones was inside and had been long deceased.

The homicide detectives arrived and, apparently accustomed to the odor, went in, found Mr. Jones, and quickly determined his death was a natural passing. (Later we learned he had died about two weeks prior.) Although it was impossible to imagine that the smell could get worse, it did when the body retrieval services arrived and began moving the man for transport. These people do this several times a day in the city and have seen every form of death, but they said they hadn't had a deceased person in such a horrible condition in years. The poor man had bloated to double his original size and was on the verge of splitting open.

Although the ravages of two weeks in the terrible heat—made worse by an oven left on—had affected the deceased far worse than others I'd seen, the investigation, body removal, and paperwork were all routine. That is, mostly routine.

Something happened to me in the man's apartment, though I didn't realize it until I got home around 2 a.m. I stripped off my fouled uniform and left it at the back door. I quickly showered, all the while amazed at how overwhelmingly fatigued I was. I attributed it to the unusual intensity of the circumstances—heat, odor, and decay of the body—that was beyond anything I'd experienced. Still, the profound exhaustion surprised me.

There was also something else, and it was extremely disconcerting. I had never felt anything like it before at any time in my private life or in any other subsequent dead body calls.

I could feel the dead man's presence.

It almost felt like he was trying to cling onto me. No, it wasn't his odor; I'm talking about his ... spirit? Yes, his spirit and I could feel it hovering over me, as if trying to possess me. It was so intense, so tangible, so overwhelming that I was on the verge of a panic attack. And I never, ever get panic attacks.

As I lay in bed, my girlfriend sleeping beside me, I fought the feeling, but it was only getting worse. A sense of being trapped and restrained seemed to be pressing me deeper and deeper into the mattress. It was such an incredibly strange and oppressive energy. I didn't understand what was happening. Why was I feeling this terrible—?

Then I knew. Just like that, I understood.

I never once felt threatened by the presence; I never thought it was going to do me harm. What I was feeling, however, and I was sure of it, was that he was seeking my help. He was trapped—not me.

I woke my girlfriend and told her about the call and what I was experiencing. She is a deeply spiritual person, almost medium like, and she immediately understood what was happening. After asking me a lot of questions about the call, what I was sensing and if I would like her to assist, she began to sink into a meditative state of deep concentration to still her mind.

She told me she sensed the spirit's energy around me, and she began to put into words things that were unclear to me. As has happened before between us, I trusted her in a realm that was unfamiliar to me and, in so doing, I could feel her calm influence. To others, this might seem strange or new age, but I knew what she was doing because I had seen her do it successfully on past occasions. She continually asked if what she was doing resonated with me and if I understood what she was saying.

I don't know how much time had passed, but I suddenly knew the spirit had left. The weight of it had lifted from me, and I could feel it gone even before she told me it was released.

Can I explain what I felt, what I knew was happening that night? No. But what I believe is that the dead man's spirit, or whatever it was, was stuck in a space between his Earthy existence and whatever else there is after. I'm convinced he was clinging to me to help him.

I never felt in danger, but I knew for sure I couldn't carry his weight for long.

EYES
By Bill Coffee

In the summer of 1981, I was a young and eager cop working out of Portland, Oregon's infamous North Precinct. The often-heard refrain on the Portland Police Bureau was, "You screw up you get sent to North Precinct graveyard shift." Happily, I hadn't messed up, but I was a newbie and working with a senior officer on day shift. I would have preferred graveyard because it was such a blistering hot summer that year. According to the National Weather Service's historical data, August 8, the day in question, was a record-breaking 107 degrees.

My partner had to go to court, so I was sent out alone with a caution from my old sergeant to watch myself. Ours was a rough beat, Portland's version of a ghetto where violence was as common as the hookers that lined the streets. But as it turned out, my problem wouldn't be any of the usual shots fired, knifings, and felony car stops. Mine would be from … well, I'm still not exactly sure.

After I told dispatch I was clear, I was sent to meet a complainant that had called in a welfare check, which was typically a "one not seen" call. This type of dispatch entailed the police knocking on the door, checking neighbors and, depending on the circumstances, forcing entry into the residence. Usually, the person in question was in the hospital or had taken an unannounced vacation. Sometimes the individual had died alone inside their home. I was hoping it wouldn't be the latter, especially on such an oppressively hot day.

The house was in a seedy neighborhood, one I recognized from a previous contact several months earlier, in which I had warned the middle-aged man about his car's expired plates. He was a Vietnam War veteran, having served in the early years of the protracted conflict. He said he was struggling with his faith and spirituality, and he told me a little about the B'nai B'rith stickers covering his bumper. As a vet, I had a soft spot for others that had served, so I just gave him a verbal warning to get his licensing squared away.

A grim-faced mailman met me on the sidewalk, and I asked him the usual who, what, and when questions, though the overgrown lawn, full mailbox, and the accumulation of daily newspapers made it clear how to proceed.

The mailman walked with me around the old, large house, and while the call was a no-big-deal situation, I remember feeling somehow grateful he was with me. He was a talker, giddily chatting about everything and nothing, no doubt thrilled by a little departure from his routine letter delivery.

We stopped at what appeared to be the kitchen window; on the inside several large, black flies flitted along the dirty sill. I knew what that meant.

Over the mailman's constant chitchat, I tried to decipher all the heavy radio traffic on my portable to see if any of the neighboring beat cars might be available to assist. Finally, I asked dispatch, and they said every North Precinct car was tied up, as was East Precinct's units. Even supervisors were taking calls. I was on my own.

The back porch was enclosed, its feeble door secured by an old-fashioned hook and eye latch. I retrieved my shotgun from my car, returned to the back porch, and quickly undid the lock, all the while the enthralled mailman watched from a distance. He remained outside as I moved through the dark doorway.

I don't know what I expected as I stepped just inside the door to the kitchen—a dead body, maybe, bloody carnage, signs of a burglary—but what I could see from where I stood, there was none of that. It was only an empty kitchen, but not for long.

One of the largest dogs I have ever seen before or since stepped into the kitchen through the far doorway. The muscle-dense beast—black and gray and unkempt—neither growled nor postured. He just stared at me, stared into my eyes so intently, so profoundly that it chilled me despite the intensive heat of the closed house.

I know now that it was an Irish wolfhound, one of the tallest of dogs, even towering over Great Danes. A dumb animal he was not. Those unblinking eyes exuded intelligence—and something else. Even today I cannot put into words what that *something* was other than to say I could see in them, well, a presence. Of what? I didn't know then and I don't know now. But those eyes and what was in them, burned into my mind.

No way did I want to force an encounter with the enormous dog, so I asked dispatch to have an Animal Control Officer come to the house and get him. The mailman stuck it out just long enough to see the wolfhound extracted from the place and witness what I had told him about the creature.

The animal didn't fight or resist Animal Control, but it never once broke eye contact with me. Even when it got turned this way and that way as the officer maneuvered him into his truck, the dog continually turned his body toward me or twisted his head about to burn me with the intensity of its eyes.

With the dog finally gone as well as the mailman, and still no backup available for me, I chambered a round into my shotgun, announced my presence, and reentered the hot kitchen. This time I went farther in than I had before the strange dog had stopped me. But I had gone only a few steps before a dreadful scene stopped me again. It wasn't another great beast, but rather a massive pool of coagulated blood that spread into an empty dining room.

I turned down my radio so as not to announce my movements, and began to stealthily follow the blood trail, which led me into a bedroom where I found yet another large pool. The blood was on a wall too, splashed crimson nearly as high as my shoulders.

Next to it, an open door.

I moved toward it, paused to listen, and then peered around the door facing into a small bathroom. The blood trail continued across the floor and disappeared through another doorway into what looked like another bedroom.

Doors make cops nervous. Much time is spent in the police academy and in ongoing training learning the safest ways to go through a door where on the other side are often surprises, some dangerous, some deadly so. We learn to go in as a team with well-trained strategy and tactics.

But I was little more than a rookie, and I was by myself. The big house and its rooms were thick with oppressive heat, stench, and filth. But my senses shut all those things out of mind, leaving only the two most needed at the moment—my ears and my eyes—both functioning at 110 percent.

I moved quickly through the bathroom, stopped at the door facing first to listen and then quick-peek around the bathroom door into the semi-dark bedroom. The blood trail led across a floor to a rancid, disgusting mattress. On it, the body of the old Navy veteran sprawled naked on his back, his mouth agape in an expression of horror, his open, dead eyes beginning to putrefy. I looked down at his neck, and I immediately wished I hadn't.

His throat was mostly gone, ripped and torn apart as if by some ghoulish fiend. A yawning opening of red shredded meat and white bone was all that remained of what once was his throat and spine. As horrific as that was, it was his eyes … that chilled.

I might have thought at that moment, at least for an instant, about the eyes being a window to the soul and all that. But there was something else about them. It was as if his eyes had looked through a portal and saw something dark and dangerous. As if they had seen hell and its tortured beings.

My training overrode these thoughts long enough to continue clearing the house. Then, not entirely sure of what I had seen, I returned to the bedroom and the obscene spectacle. When I could no longer look upon the terrible sight, I lifted my eyes to the wall behind the bed and at a framed testament from B'nai B'rith. I started to read it when—

I felt a genuine sensation of being *studied*. This was followed by an extremely heavy, dark, and oppressive energy pushing down on me. It was as if the room itself was drawing away my breath to assist the crushing weight.

So intense was this sensation that I felt compelled to leave not just the room, but the entire house, and order the medical examiner from outside away from what had occurred inside the walls.

When the ME showed up, I had to go back in and escort him through the dreadful scene. He told me that the thirsty dog had savaged the dead man's throat to seek moisture in the awful heat of the closed house.

The large blood pools were a result of how the man chose to take his life. The can of Drano he ingested had burned out his digestive tract and internal organs.

The ME confirmed that no crime had been committed, and then he left—"I'm having a busy day," he said—no doubt the result of the 107 degrees.

***

I would have many other suicides during my long police career but the accusation in those two sets of eyes, the man's and the dog's, have remained with me to this day. I understand that our minds are a powerful organ and that it's possible I underwent some form of transference of stress so common to war veterans that are expected to hide or bury entirely their emotions. But the intrusive memories and mental images that would appear seemingly from nowhere— the vivid recall of the dog, the man, and the blood— perhaps triggered by something, will not leave me. They are infrequent now, and I have put them to rest. I realize they are probably just the result of an accumulation of events over a long career.

As a street cop and a long-time member of SWAT, I faced a lot of evil during my career. But nothing like what I experienced weighting me down in that house. I'm not deeply religious, but I do have a sense of spirituality, and I'm convinced I experienced the presence of something unusual that hot day in August so many years ago, some type of evil entity.

Whatever it was, I know it was something at once dark and terrible.

DEAD MAN WALKING
By Cason Kai

It's cold in Southeast Michigan in January, bitterly cold the closer you get to Lake Erie. I was patrolling a part of an area that is busy in the summer months with boaters and tourist, but it's desolate in the deathly white of winter. One night I was carefully driving through a snowstorm on a road that leads down to the lake.

That's when I saw him, a man, walking down the road ahead of me dressed in a suit and a Fedora; the kind of hat men wore in the 1940s. Wrapped around him, a coarse, gray blanket. He walked with a purpose as if he had somewhere to go.

It was 20-degrees out, snowing hard, and the man was walking on a road where no one should be. The guy had to be mentally ill to be dressed like that in such horrific weather in the middle of nowhere. I notified dispatch that I was going to make contact with the guy.

I rolled up on him and positioned my car so he was next to my right front fender. At this distance, I could clearly see every detail of his clothing, the rough texture of his blanket, and that 70-year-old hat. I looked down to switch on my alley lights, and when I looked back up …

He was gone.

Thinking he had fallen, I got out of my car and hurried around to the other side. There was no sign of him. It was snowing so there had to be footprints; there were none. Given the terrible weather it was now a possible rescue mission, so I called for another officer to assist. We thoroughly looked everywhere, but we came up with nothing. No guy, no tracks, nothing.

I got teased a bit at the end of my shift because I had wasted so much time looking for a man who wasn't there. But I remained puzzled. I had seen him as plain as day, and then he—vanished.

At one point, a senior officer pulled me aside and gave me some backstory on the road. From the 1940s to the 1960s, the mob dumped bodies there because it was the nearest unpopulated area from Detroit. The result was that the same place where I had my experience was notorious for paranormal activity. In fact, not many officers would drive down it after dark.

It was also common for them to wrap the body in a rug or blanket.

Another officer, a retired one, told me that one time he was parked in a lot next to the same road when he saw a horse-drawn wagon pass by him. When the officer turned into the lane, it was gone. And this happened in the middle of the day.

I've always thought ghosts were supposed to be blurry and transparent. The man I saw was so clear I could see every detail of him.

Either way, that's the only one I ever want to see.

DEAD MAN'S CANE
By Kerry L. Wood

"Spirits communicate to everyone all the time, but most people are too busy to notice." ~ a medium

Roanoke, Virginia can get bitterly cold in the winter, and it's common to get 20 inches of snow. Such was the case in the winter of 1985. On the day it happened, heavy gray skies had dumped about 18 inches on us, and besides the usual closures, the city parks had been shut down for several days. While everyone else huddled around their furnaces in their homes, cops were out in the storm.

David Ragland was my partner, and we were cruising through the parks looking for anyone that might be vandalizing and stealing, as thugs are apt to do when they think they are free to act out in adverse weather. One park we checked was especially remote, and we had to plow our way through the snow to the restroom building. These structures are particularly attractive to copper thieves that go after pipes and fixtures to sell.

As we neared the building, we both heard a loud, metallic *Bang!*

Ten seconds passed. The silence was especially profound with everything under a heavy blanket of freshly fallen snow.

Bang!

There it was again.

Suspecting we had rolled up on copper thieves, we got out of our unit and approached the restroom on foot.

Bang!

Bang!

We moved to the door and listened.

Bang!

We pushed through the door ready to confront the thieves. David scanned right, and I looked left, and then our eyes fell on the only person in the deep freeze-like room. Our perception:

He was an older man lying on the floor next to the sink.

In his hand, a walking cane.

Just above him, a series of metal pipes attached to the wall.

The man was quite dead.

The banging had stopped.

We didn't know when he had died or why, but our guess was he had frozen to death. We called the medical examiner, and while we waited, we checked around outside. There were no other footprints in the fresh snow.

Later, the medical examiner told us the man had been intoxicated and dead at least 24 hours. The cause was official: He had frozen to death.

If it hadn't been for the banging on the pipes, he wouldn't have been found until days later when the snow had melted and people—children—were once again out and about.

We never heard the banging again, and we never found a logical reason for it, other than the cane the dead man clutched in his hand, where he lay, perhaps wanting desperately for someone—the police—to find him under the pipes.

A TOUCH OF THANKS
By Alexis Garcia

"Gratitude is the memory of the heart" ~ Jean Baptiste Massieu

I had completed my field-training period and had been working on my own for a few weeks when it happened. It had been a cold, overcast day, and I was working the afternoon shift, which began at 4 p.m. I sat impatiently through the sergeant's 30-minute roll call, and then I was the first one out the door, into my patrol car, and onto the street. This was my usual routine because I was always eager to get into the thick of it.

I had no sooner hit the street than dispatch broadcasted a BOL [be on the lookout] for a dark blue Nissan pickup with an unknown plate driving erratically on SR-1 highway at speeds of over 85 mph. Information was being relayed to dispatch from a motorist trying to keep up with it. I was just north of the truck and in a perfect location to watch for it, but I was no sooner in position than dispatch said the pickup was speeding by an overpass north of where I was. I quickly merged my patrol vehicle onto SR-1 and floored it to catch up.

Dispatch updated, saying the driver of the truck was still all over the lanes and using the shoulders to pass other vehicles. Just as I was gaining ground on him, a massive cloud of dust and debris erupted ahead of me on the right shoulder. I was in the far left lane, so I pulled to the side into the gravel, and anchored it. I goosed my patrol unit backward until there was an opening for me to get safely across the busy lanes to the other shoulder.

The smoke and dust had cleared enough to see that the Nissan had center punched a tree head-on so hard the thick trunk had ended up about five feet into the engine bay. The airbags hadn't deployed, leaving the driver slumped unconscious over the steering wheel.

I shouted at dispatch to send fire and an ambulance. I probably sounded panicky but I had never seen a collision so bad. I reached through the driver's window and touched the man's shoulder knowing he was in bad shape, maybe dead.

"Hey, wake up," I called to him. No response. "Hey, come on, wake up." Still nothing.

Someone ran up to help, and because it was impossible to extract the driver right then, I asked him to hold the injured man's head immobile, so I could do CPR where he sat. But the more I saw what had happened to him—the steering wheel had imbedded into his chest, and his legs were crushed—I knew he was dead. But I had to try.

Each time I compressed his chest, it felt like pushing into a bowl of mush and with each repetition blood gushed from his nose. Ambulance and fire had yet to arrive so I continued, though I knew it was useless.

When fire medics finally got there, the man was declared dead.

It was an eerie feeling seeing a dead body for the first time, let alone doing CPR on the man. My sergeant showed up and told me to work traffic control while he took photos. I slipped on my reflective vest, setup a cone/flare pattern, and began waving people through the scene.

As is always the case, some were obeying me, and others were slowing to rubberneck the crashed truck and the flashing emergency lights from the ambulance, fire rigs, and other police cars. I was guiding traffic with my left hand while holding my right along my hip. I would never have given any thought to this seemingly unimportant detail if it hadn't been for what happened right then.

Someone took hold of my right hand.

My first thought was another officer wanted to show me something or had a job for me to do. But why would he take my hand instead of my arm? I turned to see what he wanted …

There was no one there … No, there was no one within 30 feet of me.

I remember feeling chills crawl down my spine; I still get them just thinking about it. It's hard to explain, but I suddenly felt chilled. I had never experienced anything like it before and never since. It really creeped me out.

By the time I had finished directing traffic and returned to my car, I felt a sense of relief and I was surprisingly quite calm. I sat there for a moment thinking long and hard about what had just happened, and what it was that touched me. Eventually, I went back on patrol and finished my shift as usual. I didn't dare tell anyone because, well, who would believe me?

Later, I found out that the driver was a friend of a friend of mine, and he had been suffering from drug addiction. I guess some demons you can't put to rest.

What do I think I felt in the middle of the highway that night? All I know is I was busy directing traffic when someone or something grabbed my hand.

Possibly it was the driver of that pickup—his spirit—saying to me, thank you for trying.

THE SNITCH
Del Kane

Car chases are exhilarating. Dangerous, for sure, especially in heavy downtown traffic, on jammed freeways, and in school zones. Less so late at night when the streets are barren of cars and the sidewalks are deserted. But add wet roads, a cold drifting fog, and a driver armed with a gun …

Officer Thomas controlled his emotions and spoke clearly into the mic as he careened around corners in the sleeping residential neighborhood in pursuit of a fleeing dark blue sedan. Even when the driver nearly lost it and bounced off the curb, Thomas remained composed as he continued to relay his location to the other cars rushing to assist in the narrow streets. Sometimes the suspect was half a block ahead, and other times Thomas was right on his bumper. The officer didn't know the driver, but he wondered if he might be escaping to a specific location, one of these houses, maybe.

The suspect slid to a stop, sprang out the door, ran up onto a porch, and into a house. His house? A stranger's? Thomas gave his location to dispatch before following the man inside. If the suspect lived there, he had home court advantage. If it was a stranger's home, he and Thomas were on equal footing.

The house was quiet, dark; the only known factor, it was

occupied by two people—a desperate man who didn't want to go to jail and a police officer who wanted to take him there.

After Thomas cleared the living room and a small kitchen, he moved stealthily over to the entrance to a hallway and quick-peeked around the corner. It appeared to lead to an unknown number of bedrooms and bathrooms, all places that needed searching. It was eerily quiet in the house, but outside the night was filled with the wail of approaching police cars. Thomas crept around the corner and into the hall, his gun in his hand, his breathing controlled.

The man was hiding in a closet. His bullet, fired from less than 15 feet away, tore through Thomas's face.

Somehow the wounded officer returned fire, the bullet missing. The suspect shot again, the round ripping through the officer's hand. Back-pedaling toward the living room, Thomas yanked his trigger, but his rounds hit the doorframe.

The nightmare continued as the suspect moved toward him firing, but this time it was his turn to miss. Thomas shot one, two, three times, the first round hitting the man near his heart, the second slamming through his shoulder, and the third punching through his leg.

Within minutes, the formerly sleeping neighborhood was in chaos as a disco show of strobing red and blue lights from a dozen police vehicles and an ambulance bounced off the sides of houses and trees. Some officers began a high-risk coordinated sweep through the streets and yards, other officers set up perimeters two blocks out from the shooting site, ever alert for the fleeing suspect who was now wounded, desperate to escape the area, and willing to shoot anyone who got in his way.

Their flashlight beams moving about, officers checked yards and garages, in and under trees, and warned frightened neighbors to stay inside. Those not assigned an area to canvas conducted their own searches.

Such was the case with Officer Malik and Officer Kane.

By himself, Kane moved through the shadows from yard to yard, gun drawn, his eyes searching for any sign the suspect had passed through the area. Coming to the end of the block, he halted under a large tree that concealed him from view. No one could see Kane, but the yellow-orange hue from an overhead streetlight gave him a good visual of a four-way intersection. He hadn't been standing there long before he detected movement from the side of a dark house across the street. He started to inform dispatch but realized it was a cop, Officer James Malik, moving through the shadows.

Kane watched as Malik hesitated at the side of a fence, no doubt pausing to look over the open intersection before deciding what to do or where to go next.

Dispatch said Thomas had wounded the suspect, possibly multiple times before he fled the house in an unknown direction, no doubt in a haze of pain and panic. If he was hit bad and he knew he was dying, he might decide to go out with a bang. It happened all the time. Suicide by cop, it's called.

Kane noticed Malik jutting his head as if leaning forward to see something better. But he wasn't looking about at the surrounding shadows; he was looking toward the lighted intersection. A minute passed, then Malik stepped away from the house and walked down the slope of lawn to the sidewalk, all the while looking where the streetlight flooded the street.

Kane held his position, not sure what the other officer was doing. He didn't like the idea of stepping out of the shadows, let alone into a lit, wide-open street.

Malik crossed the sidewalk and stepped off the curb. He took another three steps before stopping under the streetlight. Kane observed him carefully as he tilted his head as if listening. Then

Malik nodded, and said something too low to hear. Malik listened again then snapped his head to his left. Kane was at a loss.

Malik abruptly moved out of the streetlight, crossed to a house on the far corner, and headed toward a garage, his gun leading the way. Kane stepped out from under the tree and started to cross the intersection, all the while trying to identify what the officer was seeing. Malik stopped before a shrub near the garage.

A bloody man popped up from behind the bush. He thrust his weapon at Officer Malik, but the officer was faster and sent a fatal bullet into man's body.

Once more chaos erupted in a quiet neighborhood. Police cars slid into the intersection, and an ambulance siren moaned in the distance.

It would be hours before the neighborhood was again quiet, though it would be months, maybe years, before the families would feel their lives were once again normal.

Sometime later Officer Kane was able to confer with Malik.

"How did you know where he was hiding?" Kane asked. "The suspect. How did you know?"

"How?" Malik said, puzzled at the question since he knew Kane had a full visual of the intersection from where he had been standing. "That old black man told me."

Confused, Kane asked what old black man.

"The one in the intersection, Kane. The old guy who was standing under the streetlight. He told me exactly where the suspect was. Behind that bush."

***

Note: Kane told me he had a clear and unobstructed view of the four streets, the sidewalks, and the well-lit intersection that night. He is adamant there was no one anywhere in the area. The officers talked about it at length and agreed to keep what happened just between them.

Until now.

Though shot in the head, the officer survived and retired years later after a long career.

THE COUPLE
By Melissa Davis

It was cool enough that fall night for a jacket and wet enough for rain gear, heavy rain gear. The rain was slapping my patrol car so hard my wipers were struggling to keep up.

I was working as a patrol deputy, assigned to a small county with a little over 370,000 people.

Small, but it has a reputation for over 50 haunted locations, some of which are just legends and rumor, but others are well documented.

Squinting through the rain-hammered windshield, I turned off Lone Rock Road and headed eastbound on Powell Road toward Tall Pines Park. The park's 64 acres of dense woods was quite lovely when it wasn't pouring, and I often enjoyed sitting in its parking lot to do my paperwork. A nursing home across from the park sat by itself; the closest house was about three blocks down on the opposite side of the road. One of my duties on the night shift was to close the park at dusk and to check to ensure it was clear of people, which wouldn't be an issue on such a terrible night.

Or so I thought.

I had no more pulled onto Lone Rock when my hard-working wipers revealed two people walking across the road, both wearing jackets with the hoods up over their heads. It was unusual to see anyone out at that hour, especially in a storm without an umbrella, and walking toward Tall Pines Park, of all places. So I pulled up next to them and lowered my passenger window.

"Everything okay?" I shouted over the pounding rain.

A man, late 40s, leaned in my window. "I was taking my mother for a walk," he said, "and we're headed home now."

There was something about his voice, the tone. It was so dull, almost … robotic. And they were out for a walk in a downpour?

Still leaning in the window, he added in that strange monotone, "We live in the first house on the left."

He straightened and a moment later an elderly woman's face appeared in my window. "Thank you," she said in that same dry, lifeless voice. Then she too moved away from the opening.

I rolled up the window and began to drive off. Wait—

We live in the first house on the left.

I stopped in the middle of the road. There was no house on the left. Only Tall Pines Park is on that side. I looked up at my rearview mirror.

The couple wasn't there.

I moved the mirror left and right, but I still couldn't find them. I grabbed my flashlight, got out, and shined it all about the area. They were gone. But how …? I quickly got back into my car and thoroughly checked the streets, sidewalks, and trees. Nothing.

But where could they have gone in such a short period? I had driven no more than 10 seconds after I left the couple when I stopped and began searching for them. There was simply nowhere for them to have gone in that time frame. Not into the park, not down the street, nowhere.

Later, I asked other deputies if they had ever seen the couple or if they knew anyone that lived on that sparsely populated road with that description. None of them had.

For seven more years I worked that area in our small community, and I never saw them again.

THE WARNING
By Loren W. Christensen

Police officers and just about anyone with experience in the realm of violence understand the concept of "I had a gut feeling." I had my share of them in the Vietnam War and on the city streets as a cop. But this time—a pleasant afternoon in August—the feeling was different because it came at me out of the blue when I was engaged in a no-big-deal traffic stop.

Let me illustrate the difference between what is considered a typical kind of gut feeling in police work and what I experienced on that summer day.

The previous winter, other officers and I responded to an armed robbery of a veterinarian hospital in which staff and customers, to include an off-duty cop, were forced into a large dog cage. The cop was carrying his weapon, but he was quickly overpowered and disarmed.

Just as we arrived at the hospital, dispatch told us the three armed holdup men had fled out the back door. One officer went into the hospital to gather information, and the rest of us began a coordinated search of the back lot and the connecting backyards of private residences.

There were several stacked kennels in the lot, waist-high weeds, two sheds, and an old garage. This occurred before cops called SWAT for every little thing, so the three of us searched the kennels, the small buildings, and behind a six-foot-high wooden fence surrounding the lot.

As we searched, I had this intense sensation that someone was watching us. This wasn't an unusual feeling because it fell within the parameters of the situation.

Our search ended when police units checking side streets around the hospital radioed that they had caught the suspects. The holdup men subsequently admitted to hiding in a garage loft in the next yard over, a place from which they could see our movements as we searched.

Again, there was nothing supernatural about the feeling of being watched because we were at the scene of a crime just moments after the suspects had fled.

But it was a different situation on that August afternoon on a tree-lined residential area. The day was beginning to heat up, and the neighborhood streets were quiet, probably because anyone not at work was staying inside out of the sun. There was no other traffic, no barking dogs, not even a chirping bird. Just quiet.

When a motorist blew through a stop sign like it was a green light, I pulled him over in front of a two-story white house. I never liked writing citations, figuring a simple stop and a warning was good enough to get most drivers' heads out of wherever they had been and back on the task of paying attention to the road. The driver was pleasant, apologetic, and he even thanked me.

That's when I felt it.

My heart rate suddenly accelerated, and a tingling sensation danced up my spine to bristle the fine hairs at the base of my neck. This wasn't anything new to me, as I'd felt it to greater and lesser degrees many times in Vietnam, and at least once or twice a week on high-risk situations on the police job, such as kicking in a door on a dangerous warrant service or going up against a man with a gun in a tavern. But on a pleasant summer day on a sleepy street? I bid the driver a good day and watched him pull away from the curb.

The feeling remained.

Now it was ... No, it hadn't been the traffic stop giving me the heebie-jeebies because now the feeling was growing more intense.

I made a 360-degree turn, scanning the sidewalks in all directions, as well as the streets as far as I could see north, south, west, and east. I looked over at the big house I was parked in front of and the ones on each side of it. Nothing, and I didn't see anything suspicious with the houses on the other side of the street. So why was my adrenalin accelerating?

With the fight/flight juices percolating in my veins, and with no one with whom to do battle and no threat to back away from, I headed back to my car. But before I could get there, the feeling worsened. My heart was thumping now, my eyes watering, and goose bumps were out on my arms.

I had to get in the car and do so quickly.

A lot of officers refer to their police units as their "office." For some, they think of their car as a protective shield against threats and dangers from forces outside of it. This belief is an illusion, of course, because the car doesn't protect against much of anything other than the weather. In fact, it makes for a larger target. Officers know this, but they still take some comfort once they slip inside and shut the door.

But getting into my car didn't alleviate any of the feelings. I again scanned all four sides. Nothing. Not until I accelerated away from the curb did the sensation start to lessen. Two blocks away, I pulled under the shade of a big tree and sat for a moment as my heart rate returned close to normal, my anxiety decreased, and my adrenaline began to cool.

Eventually, I returned to patrol, and my shift ended three hours later without incident.

The next day my sergeant asked me to see him after roll call.

"You stop a car on Sixty-Third and Fleet Tuesday?" he asked.

"I know nothing, and I wasn't even there," I said with a smirk. When he didn't smile at the old joke, I told the sergeant I had. "Guy blew a stop sign, and I gave him a verbal. He complaining?" I didn't understand why he would file a complaint. I was pleasant to him and—

"You stop him in front of a white house, a big one, two stories?"

"I didn't block their driveway. Did the owner…" Then I remembered the terrible case of the creeps I'd had on the traffic stop. More accurately, the rush of dread I'd had after it.

"Better sit down," the sergeant said. "A young woman came into the precinct last night. Said a uniform officer was in front of her house yesterday afternoon talking to a driver. Said her fiancé has a real hate on for the cops; he's an ex-con."

"Okay," I said, wondering where this was going.

"He saw you through the window, and apparently he flipped out. Told his girlfriend he was going to shoot you. He retrieved a rifle, loaded it, and propped the barrel on a windowsill. He lined you up in his sights and was about to fire when the woman leaped at him and tried to get the rifle away. You drove off while they were rolling around fighting on the floor. The ex-con got the weapon back, but he was majorly upset that you had left. So he beat her up pretty badly. She got away, and that's when she came here to the precinct."

I slumped deeper into the chair, struggling for air.

"Close one," the sergeant said with a shake of his head. "Be careful out there. You just used up your good karma."

THE LIGHT
By Marc Spicer

There have long been stories about Oxford Milford Road in Ohio's Butler County. Depending on whom you talk to, you will get varying accounts of what supposedly is happening, besides what you might experience there yourself. Some call it "The Legend" and others call it "The Light," but by whatever name it's the same basic story told about similar places all around the world. "Blink your headlights three times, and a light appears in the distance, then it comes toward you, only to disappear," or some variation thereof.

I never gave the one on Oxford Milford Road much credibility until a deputy and I experienced it.

Every year, especially around Halloween, we would get repeated calls up there about cars parked on the roadway and partially in people's yards. It was usually younger folks, mostly teenagers from all over as well as students from nearby Miami University that came to get spooked on the lonely countryside road. We would run them off, telling them there was nothing to see.

Occasionally, and just for the fun of it, we would head up a ways to a crossroad, turn on our spotlights, and move slowly toward the crowd. Almost every time, the kids dispersed before we got all the way to them.

One late Halloween night, another deputy and I were dispatched to Oxford Milford Road on suspicious activity at a roadway construction site. As we neared, we noticed what appeared to be someone carrying a light of some kind that emitted a weak yellowish glow. We assumed it was a "someone," though we couldn't see the figure.

Then, just like that, the yellowish light disappeared.

We scanned the area with our spotlights and got out on foot with our flashlights to look around. Not finding anyone or seeing any damage to the equipment, we cleared the call. To make sure, we did another cruise around the site before driving back up to the usual parking spots to shoo a few people away. Then it was coffee time at a little joint in Oxford.

Cops expect their lunches and coffee breaks to get interrupted, and such was the case this night. We had no more than got our cups filled when dispatch sent us back to the same construction site, on the same complaint.

Again, we saw the strange light as we pulled up to the scene, we checked the area, and once again it was gone. This time, we decided to wait out whoever it was. We positioned our cars side-by-side where we had a good view of the construction area and the nearby highway. We chatted, we watched, and chatted some more.

Then we saw a light. This one, round and brighter than the one in the construction site, was coming straight toward us. Silently.

Just as I told the other deputy that it was the quietest motorcycle I'd ever heard, or not heard, the light descended where the road dips. We waited for it to come back up ...

But it didn't.

There weren't houses or intersecting streets in the area. The road remained dark and silent.

The other deputy and I drove down to the dip, expecting to find a bicycle or a broke down motorcycle at the bottom. But there wasn't anything there. Not even marks in the grass at the sides of the road.

Up to that point, I hadn't given the urban legend any thought, as I was busy trying to figure out why we hadn't found anyone on the work site or at the bottom of the dip. We decided to head back to the construction area. The plan was I would get out on foot on the far side and check around where we had seen the earlier light.

At 0238 hours, (I still remember the time distinctly), we both saw it again, but this time the light was moving to and fro as if someone were carrying a lantern of some kind. I watched it—I assumed a male was carrying it—until it came within about 20 feet of me. Then I lit up whoever was carrying it with my flashlight.

Nothing.

He, it, or whatever it was—had disappeared. A second earlier, the light was six or seven strides away. Then it was gone. Not even a flittering firefly. Just nothing.

I radioed the other deputy and told him what had occurred. But by the time I got back to my car, he was gone. When I ran into him sometime later, it was apparent he was still shaken about what had happened. While he unsettled and confused about the whole ordeal, he said he was glad of one thing: That it was me who got so close to the light, not him.

WRONG NUMBER
By Loren W. Christensen

Writer Emma Bull wrote, "Coincidence is the word we use when we can't see the levers and pulleys." If so, where are they in this situation?

In the late 1960s, Constable Peter Moscardi worked as a police officer in England working in London. One day he ran into Dan, a friend of his who told him he had been trying to call him at work but was unable to reach him. Moscardi apologized and said his number had recently been changed. He gave his friend the new one but inadvertently mixed up the last three numbers. Instead of 116, the constable told him 661.

Several nights later, Moscardi was on patrol in an industrial area when he found an open door. He got out of his vehicle and slipped through the opening into what appeared to be an office. He looked around to see if anything had been disturbed.

A desk phone rang.

Out of impulse or compulsion, he snatched up the phone. To his amazement, it was his friend.

Shocked, Moscardi said, "Dan? What the—? How did you get this number?"

"You gave it to me the other day. You having memory problems or something?"

"I didn't give you this number," Moscardi said. "I gave you my work number."

"And I dialed it, and you answered. Funny how that works, huh?"

"But I'm not at that number I'm out on a call at an industrial site."

Confused, Dan read off the number Moscardi had given him. "That's not my number. You mixed them up."

It was at this point that the constable looked down at the telephone and, to his astonishment, saw that the phone number noted on it was the same wrong number Dan had dialed.

A wrong number given, a door left open, and a friend calling the officer at the exact moment he was standing in a building he had never been in before and in front of a phone bearing the wrong number.

Retold from an entry in *Mind and Magic: An Illustrated Encyclopedia of the Mysterious and Unexplained* (Crescent Books, 1991)

ON PATROL IN THE NEWS

St. Louis County, Missouri

On one foggy October night, a veteran officer was patrolling an area called Lemay Ferry Road when he saw what appeared to be an elderly couple walking near the Park Lawn Cemetery. It was 3 a.m.

The man was wearing a brown suit and the woman a light-colored dress, clothing hardly appropriate given the damp and chilly evening.

Officer Dicandia later told the *St. Louis Dispatch* in an interview, I honestly thought they were people visiting a grave and perhaps they had Alzheimer's. There was a nursing home close by."

When the officer saw the woman take the man's hand and the two of them walk into the graveyard, he decided to check them out. But when he turned into the cemetery—they were gone.

"That's when I got the chills," he said. "I had watched them for a good 20 to 30 seconds."

Officer Dicandia patrolled that same area for another two years but never saw them again. He is a detective now, and he still can't get the image out of his mind. "It's something I won't soon forget. I wasn't tired, and I know what I saw."

Source: *St Louis Post-Dispatch*

*

Fort Bragg, North Carolina

One night, Army officer and physician Jeffrey MacDonald stabbed his pregnant wife and his daughters, 2 and 5, to death in their home.

The house remained empty for 5 years after with boards over the windows and the power shut off. Nonetheless, military policeman Oliver Boyer and other MPs were dispatched there a half dozen times regarding mysterious circumstances.

Boyer, now the sheriff of Jefferson County in Missouri, says, "It wasn't unusual for us to get calls to the house because people saw lights on, or they heard someone talking or screaming inside the residence." He said giving credence to some of the calls was the fact the complainants were high-ranking officers on the base.

The situation reached a point where some unnerved officers refused to search the house.

Source: *St Louis Post-Dispatch*

*

California

Cindy's mother was cleaning the house when her daughter, about three years old, asked her to go to the potty with her "because there's a man in there."

The mother took her to the bathroom, but the room was empty. When she asked her daughter what she saw, Cindy told her the man was a policeman. Her mother had been a police dispatcher at one time, so she knew Cindy knew the different attires. When she asked her daughter the color of the uniform, Cindy indicated it was tan, the color of the Highway Patrol.

As they walked out of the bathroom, Cindy pointed at her bedroom, and said, "There's another one in there." She told her mother that the officers had been shot, or in her words, they had been "shooted with a shoot-gun." She then went on to tell her mother where precisely on their bodies the bullets had struck. She said one officer was hit in the elbow. As a former police dispatcher in California, the mother knew who the men were.

Later, Cindy's mother was talking to a friend of hers that still worked as a dispatcher. When she told her friend how her daughter had described the location of the officers' wounds, her friend replied that the information about one of them getting hit in the elbow was withheld from the public. Even Cindy's mother didn't know.

Note: Partners Roy P. Blecher and William M. Freeman were working out of the Woodland Area Office the night they were gunned down along Interstate 80 near the Yolo Causeway in West Sacramento. Blecher was handcuffed and shot in the back of the head and Freeman had been overpowered, shot, and killed. Investigators found signs of a struggle. Their last radio contact was at 3:12 a.m. when they stopped the suspect for a routine traffic violation. The killer was captured, tried and convicted of the murders and is currently serving a life sentence.

Source: *Your Ghost Stories, OfficerDownMemorialPage.org*

*

St. Louis, Missouri

Two officers responded to an open door and a blaring alarm at an old Victorian home in the Soulard area; the owners were out of town.

The officers entered through the kitchen, cleared it, and moved on to a room with only one way in and out. They had no sooner walked in than the door slammed shut behind them.

They continued their search throughout the house. Finding nothing disturbed, they proceeded back to the kitchen where they had been minutes earlier. This time the faucets were running.

"They were the kind of handles you had to pull up," one of the officers said later. "It gave us the chills."

Source: *St Louis Post-Dispatch*

*

New Mexico

Officer Karl Romero of the Espanola Police Department was at his post watching surveillance video aimed at various places inside and outside the station when he spotted something that spooked him.

It was a foggy figure, human in form, moving through the police parking lot and out through a locked fence.

"At first I thought it was a fly, a moth," Romero told *KOAT TV*. "But then I saw the legs. It was human," While this was the first time the video captured something, other officers at the station experienced eerie happenings that cannot be explained.

Some have said they feel someone breathing against their necks when they are working in the briefing room.

Others had heard strange noises in the station in the middle of the night and had seen "images" in the lobby. All unexplained.

The image on the video recorded by Officer Romero [you can see it on YouTube] shook many of the officers at the station.

KOAT reports that the police station, which was built in 2006, wasn't constructed on hallowed ground, and no one has died on the premises.

Source: *Fox News*

*

Massena, New York

Dragon Obretenoff [yes, that was his real name] was a Bulgarian immigrant who owned two restaurants in Massena, a small town near the Canadian border. He lost his life when a hunter mistook him for a deer.

He was buried in Pine Grove Cemetery and ever since ghost hunters have flocked to his grave.

One day a couple was walking their dog near Obretenoff's grave when they both heard someone behind them hiss, "Turn around!" They didn't, but they did flee from the cemetery, no doubt changing their dog-walking route.

There are numerous reports of electronic interference in the area to include police radios in passing police cars.

People frequently see shadow people [see Terminology page] in the graveyard, and a local ghost hunting group, as well as police officers, report seeing dark figures darting about in among the graves in the early morning hours.

Some ghost hunters believe that shadow people draw on the energy from street lamps in the area.

Source: *Listverse*

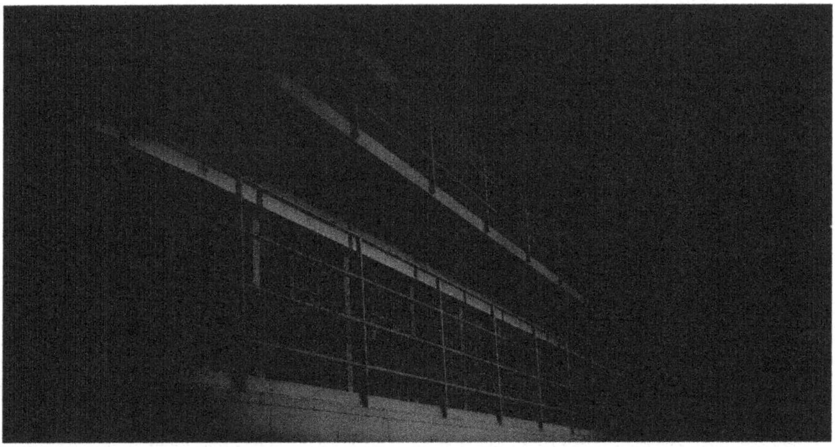

SECTION TWO

HAUNTED PLACES

JAILS AND PRISONS

Some paranormal researchers believe that there are many hauntings in jails and prisons because of the types of people incarcerated—violent, criminally insane, perverted, sadistic—as well as what the horrific years in solitude does to them. Prisoners are immediately stripped of their freedom to move about at will, to privacy, possessions, and happiness. To be confined to a small space for hours at a time oppresses the mind and body and affects one's individualism. But as Richard Pryor said after visiting an institution and witnessing first hand those incarcerated, "Thank God we got penitentiaries!"

Because of the loss of liberties and the powerful effect of spending so much time in a small room, people often experience high levels of rage and depression; some become eviler than they were before being confined. According to some paranormal investigators, when these people die in prison those intense feelings go with them and they continue to experience the same emotional troubles in their afterlife. It's for that reason people see apparitions wandering about in cells and corridors, and hear their screams and cries.

One other explanation is that because of a prisoner's profound emotional state when he dies from illness, accident, or murder, his residual energy remains. It's not an intelligent form but rather a "recording," an image or sound like an audio or video that continuously replays. Sometimes the energy weakens over time.

But other times it recharges.

GHOST PRISONER
By Joe Bertetto, GySgt USMC (ret)

I used to work the graveyard shift at the San Bernardino County Central Detention Center in California. One night, another deputy and I were sharing duties—performing all the required safety checks and working in the control room. There were always the night owl prisoners, but overall it was quieter in the wee hours as opposed to the madness of day shift.

All inmate workers were housed in an area designated as "C" tank, and I was moving along a series of what we called "officer's walkways" outside and around all of the housing units.

It was around 2 a.m., and it was my turn to complete the safety checks and initial the logs. I was moving along the walkway towards the rear of "C" tank when I had stopped to look into the housing area to see if anything was going on. As I turned back to the walkway, I noticed an inmate worker at the far end. It was routine for deputies to bring them in to sweep and mop, so I thought nothing of it and looked back into the housing area. Then I remembered something.

I didn't have an inmate scheduled out of his cell for cleaning. Did one get out of the housing area? I moved back to where I saw the man at the far end of the walkway.

He wasn't there. I looked in all directions. Nothing but quiet.

The more I thought about it, the more I realized what I had seen was a light gray presence. Then as I moved toward where he had been, the air temperature rapidly dropped as if I had just walked into a freezer. The extreme cold only lasted for a few paces before it returned to normal.

Back in the control room, I told my partner what I had just seen and felt. She believed me because she had seen similar things herself. Everyone else on the shift just laughed at me.

Jails and prisons are notorious for ghost sightings as they are a breeding ground for high emotions. Inmates lose their freedom to move, speak, and do all the things people on the outside take for granted; for sure, their world is mostly an intensely dark, depressing, and dangerous place. Many paranormal investigators that study hauntings believe the dead are attracted to such places because of the emotional charge that lingers in the air and reverberates off the cold, hard bars.

Whatever the cause, I know what I saw, and it made me a believer.

TOWER 7
By Steven Alva, LAPD, (ret)

The following incident happened while I was serving in the U.S. Army with the Berlin Brigade from 1976 through 1979. It was during the cold war with the Soviet Union in Berlin, a city divided by the great powers that won World War II.

According to the Potsdam Agreement in 1945, Berlin was divided into occupation zones, one each for the Russians, French, British, and the Americans. It was during this time the Americans carried out the only military ceremony with the Soviet Union. It took place in Spandau Prison in the British sector of the occupation.

The prince of Prussia built the structure in the 1840s to confine his political rivals and anyone else he deemed to be a subversive. A hundred and thirty-five years later, it still looked like an old medieval castle that Hollywood would create for a horror movie. It was built with 5-foot-thick brick and mortar walls to stop cannon balls, and a large wood and steel gate that lowered to seal the main entrance. The Gestapo took it over during World War II and used it to hold prisoners, conduct interrogations, and to perform executions.

When I was there, it was a dark, cold, and drafty place, befitting of its only prisoner, Rudolf Hess, Deputy Fuhrer to Adolph Hitler. Sentenced to Spandau in 1947, Hess would spend 40 years there and then, at the age of 93, commit suicide.

For sure the prison had a long and bloody past, and God only knows what horrors were committed there. The British soldiers stationed nearby knew it to be haunted and avoided the place like the plague.

During my tenure, someone from my command headquarters decided to put together a unit of combat veterans to participate in a ceremony with the Russian honor guard. The idea was to show them up and let them see what experienced infantry soldiers looked like, as opposed to their more ceremonial approach.

Each of us was hand-picked and we practiced every single aspect of the ceremony over and over until we were all sleeping at attention. It paid off because when the day came, we outshined the Russians. But as usual, there was a flip side: We had to remain and the Russians, who were as frightened of the bloody place as the rest of us, got to leave. Only Hess's doctors remained. For three months, we lived in the compound and pulled prison guard over the old Nazi.

There were nine guard towers around the prison wall. We would enter the base of a tower through a locked door and climb a steep ladder-like staircase to a trapdoor under the floor of a guard stack. Once inside, we would close the small door and stand on it throughout our watch. All the towers were the same, that is, except for Tower 7.

That one was—special.

Whenever we had to pull guard in Tower 7, the others would ask the next morning if anything happened. I think everyone had experienced something strange there. Did it have anything to do with the French soldier who hung himself in it years earlier?

One day it was my time to pull a shift in the infamous tower. As usual, the sergeant of the guard marched fresh troops to each post. When we got to Tower 7, located at the rear section of the prison, the sergeant unlocked the ground level door, I worked my way up the steep staircase, climbed into the guard shack, closed the trapdoor, and assumed my post as the door far below was once again locked.

I had been there just a short while when two strange things happened simultaneously. I heard the door at the base of the tower open, and I felt the temperature drop. The door opening at that moment was strange because it wasn't the end of my shift, and only the sergeant of the guard had the key.

Then I heard heavy, labored breathing as if someone were having trouble getting air. But it was the next sound that turned my blood cold.

Footsteps. On the stairs. Ascending toward me.

I called out, "Who goes there? Stop and identify yourself!" I had a full magazine of live ammunition, and I thought about loading my weapon. But I stopped myself.

The footsteps grew nearer until they were just under the floor of the guard shack.

Then something pushed up against the trapdoor on which I was standing.

I could hear what sounded like someone mumbling something, all the while the trapdoor bumped up and down and continued to do so for several minutes. I was so petrified and I—

It stopped. Then quiet.

The next day when the guys asked if anything had happened on my post in Tower 7, I just told them no.

Three months later, we were all glad to leave the unsettling place known as Spandau Prison. So many people had lost their lives there in such terrible ways. I was happy to be gone, and I never looked back.

I guess the German people of Berlin felt the same way after Hess died in 1987. They demolished that brick and mortar house of horrors and by doing so freed, I hope, all those trapped and tormented souls.

THE ETERNALLY CARING NURSE
By Dwayne Howie

My career in corrections began after serving Uncle Sam in two separate branches of the military. Years of military service plus a career in the hard, gray, and unforgiving environment of a prison system tends to make a person see things realistically and discard anything that is nonsense. That's why what I'm about to tell you blew my mind.

The East Coast facility opened in 1900 as a tuberculosis hospital. In the early 1980s, the structure was remodeled into a prison, with housing for minimum and medium security inmates, as well as a medical wing to tend to injuries and a variety of illnesses.

I have many fond and not so fond memories of those convicts commuted to natural life sentences after the state removed the death penalty. Their elation didn't' last because it was reinstated a short while later. Many inmates died from illnesses related to HIV and AIDS before modern medications began to save lives. Others died from TB and, of course, there were the inevitable suicides (many others attempted it but failed).

For the 20 plus years I worked in the institution there were questions from inmates in the medical section about seeing a black female nurse dressed in red and pink striped clothing. They said they saw her bring water and sometimes food to the ill men. The first time an inmate told me about her I assumed he was on psychotropic meds or some other kind that caused visions or hallucinations. But then other inmates began telling me the same thing. No matter how often I informed them that no one in the medical department wore that type of uniform, the reports of sightings continued. I never saw the "nurse" on any of my shifts, but I began to wonder that there might be something to it when inmate after inmate told the same story.

They couldn't all be hallucinating. Could they?

The facility closed in 2008. I had retired by then, but I had one last opportunity to tour the old building. It was in good shape for a structure over 100 years old, and so very hauntingly empty, though in my mind all those many incarcerated lives still occupied the place.

As we walked down long empty halls and passed through bare rooms, I could still hear those old bumps, creaks, and other odd sounds I had always attributed to pipes and regulators so common with steam heated buildings.

But steam no longer passed through the pipes.

We worked our way up to the third floor, a place never occupied by inmates, though the night shift officers still had to check it each shift. They frequently told me about hearing sounds of someone walking behind them or hearing doors closing in areas they had just secured and locked.

There was a story at that time about a patient housed on the third floor back when it was a TB hospital, years before it was a correctional facility. The man killed himself by jumping off a balcony; a rope looped around his neck stopped him before he hit the floor. We never knew his real name, so the correctional staff referred to him as "Sam."

Touring that third floor we could hear Sam again—those odd

sounds that couldn't have been steam in the pipes.

As the tour ended, one of the other men in the group, a friend and past coworker at the correction facility, told me to follow him. I did, wondering why he seemed anxious and jittery. He showed me an old slide carousel and projector he had found in a storage area. After setting it up, he proceeded to flip through pictures of the facility taken back when it was the TB hospital. There were lots of slides from the 50s and 60s of people, patients, and cars in the big parking lot. Then came the pictures of which he was so anxious.

"You remember that nurse the inmates always asked about, the one who would get them water and food?" When I said I did, he adjusted the slide carousel. "Ready to see something?"

Then he began to show me slide after slide of a nurse—the same nurse all the inmates had described in vivid detail. In some, she was standing with adult patients and in others with pediatric patients. There were a few of her posing with doctors and friends. All taken at the hospital so long ago.

I didn't know what to think. Did all those men who kept asking about her see an apparition? A ghost? It was very creepy.

Over the low hum of the slide projector, I could hear those bumps, creaks, and other odd sounds.

SOME STAYED BEHIND
By Loren W. Christensen

To better understand the intricacies of paranormal research, *Sapulpa Herald* reporter Brian Patrick was permitted to do a sort of "ride-a-long" with investigators from Sooner Paranormal of Oklahoma. Their target was the former Creek County Jail in Sapulpa, Oklahoma. There had been rumors for some time about a restless spirit in the old facility and Jim Pace, founder of the organization, was called in to evaluate the property.

According to Pace, who brings a massive amount of paranormal investigative experience to the task, the scientific approach is key to revealing genuine evidence rather than relying on superstitious conjecture. It's also important, he says, to know the history of a place. Besides the incredible negative energy that typically exists around any structure used to incarcerate violent and troubled souls, Pace learned that a deputy sheriff was accidentally shot and killed in the jail shortly before the facility moved to a new location. Some people believe his spirit still walks there.

Pace likes to first map a site to better track any paranormal activity. He says, "When we map a location, we use grid paper to draw a representation of the home, business, or property to know precisely where we are recording or filming. We assign numbers to each room we investigate, noting areas on our drawing of reported activity. This system helps us later when we review our work."

It also allows the investigators to more easily point out to the client where they uncovered activity. Additionally, should the team conduct a follow-up investigation, they have a record of where to concentrate their efforts.

Sooner Paranormal of Oklahoma investigators employ something called a Gauss meter to detect any fluctuations in electromagnetic energy in a location. A base level is first established by measuring inside and outside of a target building. If the Gauss meter shows a spike during an investigation, it indicates a possible presence. Pace's people are always careful to stay away from electrical conduits.

The crew also uses video equipment and motion sensors to disclose movement in a specific area and observe images better on the equipment.

When the investigation is over, the real work begins as the crew evaluates their findings, a process that can take hours. The team found the following after only one investigation.

When they checked the second floor for EVPs, electronic voice phenomena, (see "Terminology" page), they captured one.

An investigator asked the empty room, "Is it okay to shoot pictures in here?"

"Shoot me," the recorded voice replied.

They discovered one room had random spots that were colder than the rest of the area.

A photograph revealed a cluster of four orbs in one corner.

Perhaps the most dramatic moment of the night happened when both Pace and the reporter, Brian Patrick, felt a tightening of their throats when they neared a door to one of the rooms.

Pace's conclusion of the evidence gathered from the one

investigation was that the old jail might not be haunted, "but there was definitely paranormal activity in the place."

In fact, Patrick was so impressed that he and his wife joined the paranormal organization, and did excellent work with them for eight months.

"The difference between a believer and skeptic," Jim Pace says, "is a personal experience."

THE DRAWING
T-MINUS 1 HOUR, 46 MINUTES
By R. S.

I lost my father to lung cancer on February 16, 1999. If anyone had asked about my thoughts concerning the afterlife at that time, I probably would have told them that once you're dead, that's it. No heaven, no hell, no singing angels, just nothing. As a patrolman with almost five years on the job, I was used to seeing dead and dying people. It has a way of making you a realist and maybe a cynic as well.

Not long after losing my father, a co-worker told me about a TV program called *Crossing Over* starring John Edward, a medium. I watched the show, but I wasn't sure if it was real. No one talks to the dead, do they? I bought Edward's book *One Last Time* and read it with an open mind. It was hard getting through parts of it without becoming teary-eyed, and the more I read, the more convinced I was that communicating with the afterlife could be real. I went on to read other books about mediums and anything pertaining to psychic development.

Although my interest in mediumship and communication with the deceased was relatively new, I have had a lifelong interest in other areas of the occult and pretty much anything else out of the ordinary.

Around 2000, my police agency went to permanent shifts. I ended up on the graveyard shift, which gave me time on quiet nights to read some of my books and practice psychic development. One simple exercise I liked was to have someone think of a color while I tried to guess it.

I soon discovered I could do it fairly well, though I was better able to connect with some people than with others. For example, my friend Joe and I hired on the job at the same time. Our connection was such that I usually could correctly guess whatever color he was thinking. It even got to the point where he would whisper his chosen color to someone and say, "Watch this." More times than not I would guess it correctly.

On September 11, 2001, I was working inside, assigned to a job we called "doorman," which consisted of booking in new prisoners and checking on those already in custody. Joe was the desk officer that same morning. I don't remember if the night was busy, but I do remember it was a quiet morning.

It was around 7 a.m. when I thought I'd take advantage of the quiet and try my version of remote viewing [see "Terminology" page], which our government spent millions on in a secret program in the early 1990s. There are many variations as to how to do it. My method was to ask Joe to think of a place, anyplace, but don't say aloud what it was or where it was. Then he was to choose a random number, which he would tell me.

While the secret location he held in his mind was somewhere on the planet, his chosen random number gave me a focal point on which to focus. In other words, instead of thinking about the entire world, I concentrated only on the number. Think of it as how a bloodhound uses a piece of clothing to zero in on, say, a missing child, as opposed to focusing on an entire forest.

I then used what is called "automatic writing" [see "Terminology" page] to draw an image, or what many regular remote viewers called a "pictogram."

When Joe told me he was ready, I quieted my mind and let my pen go on its own without me consciously thinking about what my hand was putting down on paper.

When the time was up, my hand, that is, my subconscious mind had drawn what looked like two buildings, one with a line into it and the other with an angular shape off to its side.

When Joe saw what my hand had produced, he said, "Nah, I was thinking about the Empire State building." Then he added, "But I did think about the Twin Towers for a moment."

At that point, I didn't think my picture resembled either. We finished our shift and went home at 8 a.m.

At 8:46 a.m., the United States was shaken to its core by the worse terrorist attack in modern history. I turned on my television and watched as one of the towers burned before a second plane slammed into the other.

My phone rang. "The towers!" Joe said. "You drew them! ... but now ... they're not there."

I looked at my drawing. Now I understood it. One building I had drawn with a line into it and the other with an angular shape off to one side without a line. But I could see now that the figure was ...

... a plane pointed at the second building.

HOSPITALS

Google "hospital spirits," and you find links to sites ranging from "haunted hospitals," to blogs written by nurses telling of their experiences with the spirit world in the halls of working hospitals and those long-closed.

One blogger nurse warns that if people could see what she sees of the spirit world in hospitals, pregnant women would never birth their children in them. To paraphrase: It doesn't make sense to deliver a child in a place where sick people and old people die. If there are no other options, at least first purify the space of wandering spirits, dark emotions, and thoughts.

Then there are hospital security officers, men and women that patrol the busy corridors during the day, as well as at night when lighting is dim and shadows deep.

They too have their stories.

NURSE BETTY, THE "HAINT"
By Hock Hochheim

"Haints" is a deep southern or East Texan word for ghosts.

Haint ain't in the dictionary, but back when this incident took place, it was in the mind of many a Texan, especially those familiar with that great monolith atop the hill. I say many a Texan but not me. I was a total skeptic. In fact, I was such a skeptic I was even skeptical of my skepticism.

That is, until that one night when I experienced something up on that hill I never had before and never have since.

The great building was once a major medical facility called Flow Hospital, and it reigned supreme high above the center of Denton. Both my kids were born there, and nurses wheeled me around in those halls whenever I got busted up as a cop. I fought prisoners inside the place, as well as out on the grounds, and I also investigated shootings, suicides, and killings in and around the parking lots.

Over time, modern hospitals sprang up around town, and ol' Flow began to lose business. Owners changed, but that didn't help. It shut down, and not long after it was empty. Someone or maybe a business or corporation owned it then, and they hired our police department to work security in the mostly empty building; the front office stayed open evenings and nights for a while.

Other officers and I worked it three or four times a month for years, an easy overtime gig that cops everywhere have always loved. Mostly we walked the halls of the three-story building, which included a morgue and a basement. It was a perfect setting for a horror movie, especially at 2 a.m. on a winter's night.

Between foot patrols, officers watched TV on small camper-style sets brought from home. When I wasn't working patrol, I wrote a lot and even practiced my karate katas. It was the 1980s, and it was an easy gig.

Easy, except for Nurse Betty.

She was a young nurse who worked at the hospital years earlier, a real beauty who caught the attention of many of the doctors. But she fell head-over-heels for one, and since he was already married, they began to date secretly. Then Betty became pregnant at a time when abortion wasn't legal. So one night the doctor aborted his own child without the assistance of nurses. Without the right instruments and equipment available to him, he was unaware that Betty was bleeding internally. She died in an elevator before she and the doctor had reached the first floor.

Soon after, Betty began to haunt the halls of Flow Memorial Hospital. All the veteran nurses and doctors knew about the ghost but because I was a skeptic, I ignored it.

Until something happened to me too.

It was a warm summer evening when I walked into the first-floor office, clicked on the TV, and spread several detective cases onto a big desk. I gathered up a handful of reports, stepped into a supply room right off the main office, and headed over to a copy machine. I opened the lid, put in the paper, and hit the button. It was a routine I had done many times before. But this time …

Three things happened at once.

I experienced a total body, spine-tingling chill that took my breath away.

I knew someone was behind me.

It touched my back. But yet it didn't.

I spun around, but the thing in the corner of my eye moved too, staying behind me, over my shoulder, and just a hair-width out of sight. I saw something, but I didn't. I couldn't have, but I did.

I spun about twice in front of the copy machine. Twice, like an idiot.

Then the feelings—the electric tingling and the bone-numbing chill—were gone. Gone as fast as they came.

"What in the hell was that?" I said out loud to no one. No one?

I gathered up my papers and returned to the desk trying to shake off those terrible feelings, ones I'd never had before and would never have again. Up to now, I wasn't concerned about the hospital ghost or any other haints for that matter. Not even on the lowest subliminal level.

I would work overtime there for years, long after they shut down the front office and moved our headquarters into the empty basement emergency room. Even with Nurse Betty's legend and my supply room experience, I continued to walk the halls of that building in the dead of night, never once having that feeling again. You would think after my unsettling experience I would be mentally predisposed to feel something, but no. It came only once when I was completely and thoughtlessly un-predisposed to the idea.

Years later, an officer wandering the halls at 3 a.m. heard weird noises and went searching. No haints that time but rather three burglars, which he caught singlehandedly. I was impressed, not just because he wrangled three bad guys by himself, but because the officer heard weird noises in a suspected haunted building, and like Scully and Mulder in the *X-Files*, he pulled his gun and flashlight and went forth to investigate.

I only had one file in my personal x-files: that supply-room experience. I was open then, and I still am to any explanation from any pro in the paranormal field as to what happened that evening. Haint? Dizzy from allergies? What I can say for sure is that I had zero agenda, no dog in that hunt. It was just *weird*.

Eventually, they ripped the structure down, and replaced it with a University of North Texas dormitory.

I wonder where Nurse Betty is now?

Still haunting those grounds?

HOSPITAL MORGUE
By Colleen Formanek

I worked security at two local hospitals before I became a police officer. One of my many duties was to oversee conditions in the basement morgue. It made me a little nervous at first, but it helped that the job was simple: check the temperature of the room every few hours, transport the deceased from their hospital rooms to the morgue, and process paperwork. One night when I was still new, my superior said I had earned my stripes and was ready to work by myself. She advised me that officers at shift change had lodged two bodies in the morgue.

After completing my indoor patrol, I headed down to the basement to make a morgue check. The architects must have had a sense of humor because they had enhanced the creep factor by designing the hallway to the cold room to be dark and maze-like. Once inside, I checked over the "body roster," opened the heavy door to the walk-in cooler and—froze in place.

Something was inside with the two bodies

It was a dark shadow figure, six-foot tall, yet I could see through it, and it was bending over one of the bagged bodies.

I remained motionless as a thousand goosebumps spread over my arms. And I was suddenly cold, more intensely than the temperature in the cooler.

Seconds passed before I could shut the cooler door, rush out of the morgue, and securely lock the outer door behind me. Shocked and in disbelief of what my eyes had truly seen, I hurried down the hall to get away from that room.

Because I was new and I didn't know my supervisor well, I decided not to say anything. But after a few weeks of getting comfortable with her, I took a chance and described what I had seen that night. After my story, she smiled and then laughed. Does she think I'm crazy? I wondered.

"Don't worry," she said. "You'll have plenty more experiences like that working in this place." Then she added these words.

"Understand this. A hospital is a gateway between the living and the dead. We've all had things happen to us here."

One night, sometime after my experience in the morgue, I was called to remove the body of a man who had just died. My shift partner hated going anywhere near the morgue because of an experience he once had and would never talk about. But I needed help, so I called him on the radio to meet me in the patient's room.

I retrieved a gurney and got there first, noting the refreshment cart in the hall outside the door. The cart typically indicated someone was about to pass on, and the hospital was kindly offering something for the family and friends that had gathered to say their goodbyes.

Because the curtains were closed around the man's bed to allow the bereaved a little more time, I went over to the nurse's station to pick up his paperwork. I asked a nurse how long she thought the family would be and she said they had all left about an hour earlier.

My partner still hadn't made it to the floor, so I wrestled the cart inside the room and pushed aside the curtain. Whoops. An elderly man, a friend or a brother, was sitting on the couch, his head in his hands.

"Oh," I said. "Sorry. I was told everyone had ..."

I closed the curtain and quickly stepped back, bumping into the nurse who had come to help me transfer the body.

"What's wrong," she asked. "Why did you step back like that?"

"There is still a family member in there with him. He's mourning. I wanted to give him some more time and privacy."

"What?" She pushed past me and pulled the curtain open. "No one is in here. See?"

The sofa was empty; on the bed lay a zipped closed body bag.

At first, I was startled. Where had the man gone? Then I could feel something there in that space, some ... presence. Yes, a presence, and I knew, I could feel, that it was ... watching.

My partner finally showed up, and the nurse left. After we wrestled the bag over onto the gurney, I asked him to wait a second. Because of what I had seen in the morgue and just now on the sofa, I felt a compelling need to look into the body bag. I slowly zipped down far enough to move the material aside to see the face.

I sucked in my breath. It was the man I had seen sitting on the couch a few minutes earlier.

I looked up at my partner. "I ..." I struggled to collect myself. "I wanted to see—"

"I know," he said, as if he knew what I was going to tell him. "I've had the same thing happen to me." His eyes moved around the partially curtained off area.

"Let's get outta here," he said. "We're being watched."

OTHER HAUNTED PLACES

To state the obvious, each person has a distinct personality, life experiences, interrelationships, and so on. Many paranormal investigators believe the individual takes these elements with them when they die, meaning that each encounter with a spirit is unique because of what the deceased has retained after death. Likewise, the location of the spirit or ghost presence is also distinctive.

Why is one place haunted and another not? Sometimes it's based on the spirit of the deceased and its reasons to remain in a specific location. Other times, there is no clear reason, at least not to the living.

Hotels, apartments, hospitals, factories, and prisons that have had a long history of occupancy—and all the fluctuating physical pain and emotions that go along with the human condition—are more likely to be haunted than, say, newly constructed sites.

Which brings up these questions.

Why has this five-story apartment building constructed in the late 1800s never had a reported haunting?

Why is this house haunted, in which an elderly woman died of influenza, while this house over here, where someone butchered an entire family, not affected at all by ghosts and spirits?

Why does it seem that there are so many hauntings where

someone passed 80 years ago when millions have died since without associated paranormal events?

Who knows? No one, which is why the study of the paranormal is at once frustrating and fascinating. That said, many paranormal investigators feel that spirits remain in specific locations so they can let the living know their story. They often do this by making noises or moving objects. Sometimes the strange sounds or the relocated things are specific to the person who passed, such as a hairbrush, book, or tool. These actions might be done to alert a loved one, while other times they are experienced by strangers and people who don't believe in the paranormal (that is, the people didn't use to believe).

Some paranormal investigators believe that while we often associate hauntings with houses, statistics show they occur more frequently in other locations. This is because, as some investigators contend, spirits need abundant energy to be seen, but the average home doesn't provide enough. Therefore, larger places, such as museums, churches, hotels, offices, and other locations that produce a lot of energy, are more likely locations for hauntings.

It's believed that sensitives are better able to experience an invisible presence or see a visible one, even when a location has been declared free of them. Some experts claim a cemetery is the last place to find a spirit, but some sensitives can see and feel them on the grounds and in the mausoleums.

One paranormal investigator made a list where he has found the most hauntings, the first one being the greatest and the last one the least. Remember, this is just one sensitive's experience. Not all are the same.

- Battle sites, such as Civil War fighting locations
- Places where disasters or mass killings have occurred

- Hospitals
- Jails and prisons
- Houses with a history of violence and emotional strife
- Graveyards

COFFEE AND CUPS
By Loren W. Christensen

It had been called skid row forever, but in the mid-1980s Portland's politicians and developers began referring to the 12 square blocks of rundown buildings, flops houses, gin dives, and wino-populated sidewalks as Old Town. The name didn't change the horrid place where so many down and out men and women wasted away from cheap wine and bad dope, slept in doorways every night, fought the cops and each other with fists and broken bottles, and bled out on rundown sidewalks and potholed asphalt.

Beneath this wretched part of Portland that many a beat cop called "the place forgotten by God," lies what the historians called Underground Portland, a series of catacombs and tunnels winding about just below skid row, er, Old Town. From 1850 to the beginning of World War II, the tunnels were used during the days to deliver goods to businesses from ships in the harbor. But after the sun went down, they were used for drugs, illegal booze, prostitution, gambling, and human trafficking. Many a man's drink was drugged, and after losing conscious the hapless soul was dropped through a trapdoor into one of the tunnels. When he awoke, he would find himself at sea, having been sold to the highest bidder among various captains. Not all men survived; many died in the tunnels.

Bill and I had just cleared the precinct and were on our way to morning coffee when dispatch changed our plans with a burglary call "with curious circumstances" at Allan's Café, Second and Davis Street. It's not good to keep cops from their morning caffeine, but duty called.

Allen's was one of many new businesses springing up in Old Town, which was part of the city's renewal plan to spruce up the area and hopefully capture business from the wealthy folks who worked in the high rises in the city's core area. We had cruised by the place a few times and had intended to stop by and introduce ourselves, but until now we hadn't had the opportunity. The small storefront, located at one corner of the building, had been empty for as long as I could remember, its windows too dirty to see in, and its inset doorway urine splashed and strewn with litter.

"That must be the complainant," Bill said, as I pulled us to the curb in front of Allen's. The 30-something man was standing in the entryway, his arms crossed, hands cupping his elbows, and his weight shifting from one leg to the other. "Seems wrapped a little tight."

I greeted him as we got out of our unit, but the man didn't acknowledge it and continued with the elbow cupping and swaying, his eyes large and … frightened? Bill looked over at me and raised his eyebrows.

Only a few people were out and about on the sidewalks. Halfway down the block a sandwich board near the curb read "Tours: Portland Shanghai Tunnels, Daily At 2 P.M."

"You call?" Bill asked. The man made a short nod. "About a burglary?" The man nodded again.

Someone had done a nice job cleaning up the exterior of Allen's with fresh jade-green paint, new windows, and red lettering that read: Allen's Café. Good Coffee. Fresh Pastry. Big Sandwiches. Conversation.

The large south and west side corner windows were covered with heavy steel security bars. The new-looking door was edged with multiple locks, and an open steel security door was positioned against the side of the inset. I looked back at the man. If this was Allen, he wasn't terribly conversational.

"You okay, sir?" I asked. It wasn't uncommon to find burglary victims shaken from having an intruder invade their space. Psychological rape, one victim called it.

His eyes came into focus and blinked as he looked from me to Bill and back to me again. "Yes. Yes, I'm sorry. I had a bit of a …" He turned about and led us inside the place. "Come in, please. I'll show you." Bill asked his name. "I'm Allen St John. I own the café."

It was a tiny place: four tables and a long bar-type table by the window, hanging plants, and an order station. It wasn't more than 40 feet by 40 feet.

"There," the man said, still hugging himself as he pointed with his chin toward a pile of white coffee mugs on the floor. No, not a pile, but rather a careful arrangement of about two dozen mugs centered on the floor between the four tables. They had been arranged into a small pyramid, four cups on each side, then three, then two, and one at the top.

I looked at the man. "Why are they—?"

"I didn't put those there," he breathed. He pointed at other cups lined up on shelving behind the register. "I keep them there. After they're cleaned, I put them there so I can easily retrieve them when customers come in."

"The front door forced?" Bill asked rhetorically. I saw him look at the door facing the same as I did when we entered. There wasn't any indication of tampering. The man shook his head. "How about the back door?"

"There isn't one."

"The cups were like this when you came in," I said. "When did you come in?"

"About thirty minutes ago. I left last night at about seven. I cleaned up, swept, did dishes, and locked the front door and security door when I left. You can see how strong the doors are. And the windows are barred, and they don't open anyway."

"No other way to get in?" Bill asked.

"No officer," Allen said impatiently. "This room is it. There's no way anyone could hide in here when I was closing up. I don't even have a restroom. Besides they'd have to unlock both doors to get out and I have the only keys. And they were locked tight this morning just as I left them last night."

He glanced over at his coffee machine where a full pot of coffee and another of clear water steamed. He looked back at me and swallowed. "I didn't do that."

"Didn't do what?" Bill asked. "Make the coffee?"

Allen pulled his arms in tighter against his chest and looked at my partner with impossibly large eyes. He shook his head. "I ... I open at nine thirty. I don't make coffee until just before then." Without turning his head he looked over at the pots, then back at Bill as if too afraid to look there longer. "It was ... steaming when I came in at seven thirty."

My read on Allen, and Bill concurred later, was that he wasn't mental, but he definitely was a very frightened man.

"Anything taken?" Bill asked, pulling out his little notebook.

He shook his head. "No. Just things ... disturbed. Those cups piled like that and ... the coffee."

We got Allen's information and headed for the car. Bill wrote the report noting that it was a burglary with property moved about but nothing was taken. With so many burglaries called in each day, the detectives mostly paid attention to those with property stolen and suspect information. Allen's report no doubt worked its way to the bottom of the pile and was eventually turned into nothing more than a computer entry in the system.

Allen's Café didn't last and a few months later the corner space was again empty.

Tunnel tours, their tales of vice, crimes, death, and hauntings therein continue to this day.

Note: I recently caught the tail end of the TV program *Ghost Adventures*. It was a rerun of the 2012 opening season of the program in which they were investigating Portland's tunnels. They experienced doors rattling, a ghostly heat signature on one of their instruments (probably an infrared motion detector), and an EVP near a prostitute's cove in the tunnel, saying, "Let's get naked."

THE STABBER
By Kasey Keckeisen

Like most cops, I am skeptical by nature. I've always been interested in the supernatural, and I love horror movies, but I've never seen a ghost nor do I wish to. I never saw one the night I'm going to tell you about, but my partner did, and I trust what he told me just as I've trusted him with my life many times. No, I wasn't there for the ghost sighting.

But I was there for the creation of the ghost.

It happened about 12 years ago, and I distinctly remember the incident because it was one of my first as a SWAT operator in a major metropolitan police department in Minnesota. It started out as a typical domestic disturbance call. But when the first patrol officers arrived, one of the male participants threatened them with a knife. A moment later, he plunged the knife into his own body, then quickly barricaded himself inside his home. In a matter of seconds, the call accelerated from a family fight to an armed barricaded subject with hostages. Shortly after, my SWAT team rushed to the scene.

We quickly replaced the patrol officers and took position behind a large oak tree on the corner of the lot that allowed us to watch the front of the house and one of its sides. We held this position as an incident command (IC) post was set up, and the hostage negotiator began to communicate with the volatile man inside. In time, the hostage taker allowed the hostages to walk out, which left us to deal with the suspect.

Over the course of the standoff, we learned the family had been trying to do a sort of intervention on the man who was off his meds, violent, and suicidal. The attempt had deteriorated and that is when the police were called.

At one point, I saw a face matching the description of the man peer out from between the curtains covering the living room window. I radioed IC and told them I had had a visual on the guy, but he had disappeared. A few minutes later, a light in a small upstairs window came on, and I radioed it in. This went on for hours: A face would appear in the window, and I'd radio it in. A light in the upstairs bathroom window would come on and go off, and I'd radio it in. The face would appear again in the window, and I'd radio it in.

Then the light stayed on in the upstairs bathroom. We waited. But there was no further movement in the house, no more glimpses of the man's face in the window, and no more conversation between him and our negotiation team.

But still, we waited.

Finally, the order came for SWAT to make entry.

We stacked up, streamed in, and swept one room at a time. We found the man upstairs.

He was lying in the bathroom, and every square inch of its white-tiled walls and floor was dripping blood.

The man had cut his neck, not by drawing the knife across the front, as is the norm, but by plunging the blade into his throat over and over. He rammed it in, pulled it out, rammed it in again, pulled it out, and he continued to do so until he had lost so much blood he could no longer go on. With all the connective tissue cut away, his head had flopped back like a depressed Pez dispenser.

I'm sure even the veteran SWAT operators were stunned by what had to have been some kind of internal demons that drove the mentally disturbed man to do this to himself. A mere slice across the arteries would have killed him within seconds, but he had stabbed himself repeatedly until he finally succumbed to the loss of blood.

We cleared the rest of the house and went back outside. IC had debriefed the family about the death and we had no sooner exited the house than they began screaming at us.

"It's your fault," they shouted. "Why did you let him die? You made him do it with your shiny guns."

They were Native American people, and they commenced to chant and burn sage, an ancient ritual that is performed to cleanse negative energy and ward off evil spirits. Why I wondered, did they have sage with them?

10 years later
My friend, also a SWAT officer at the time of the suicide call, was now working as a K-9 officer. One day we were both in training, and he said, "You're never going to believe this, but beat officers and I have taken numerous break-in calls at that house where the guy nearly decapitated himself."

My buddy and his K-9 partner went along with the primary unit because if the intruder fled, he and his dog could quickly get on the hot trail. But every time the officers responded, there was never any indication anyone had left the house or, for that matter, had even been inside. One night my friend had grown impatient with it all.

"We've been here four times in the last three weeks about someone breaking in," he said to the complainant. "There is never anyone here or any sign someone entered. Why do you keep calling us?

The complainant looked embarrassed and said the officers wouldn't believe his story. He was urged to tell them anyway.

"Ok," the man said, taking a deep breath. "I'll be alone down here in the living room watching TV. The light will go on in the upstairs bathroom. When I go to check it out there is no one there. So I turn it off and go back downstairs. Then the bathroom door will slam shut."

The man took another deep breath. "I try to put it out of my head, and I tell myself I'm just imagining things. But then out of the corner of my eye I'll see a guy come out of the bathroom, come down the stairs, and go behind the curtain over there by the front window.

That's the same window I saw the man looking out of 10 years earlier. The upstairs bathroom is where we found him.

"I freak out," the complainant said, "and run out of the room. But as I do, I hear the door to the upstairs bathroom slam shut again. I figure there is someone in my house messing with me, right? So I call the cops. But when you guys show up you never find him."

My friend asked the man what he knew about the history of the house

"It's been in my family for a while. I bought it from my cousin."

"Listen, sir," my friend said, "No one is breaking into your house and you're not crazy. But you really need to talk to your cousin about its history.

**

As I said in the beginning, I'm a skeptic by nature but I still I wonder about what was happening in that house.

Did an evil spirit take hold of the man all those years ago?

Could a possession have shown itself as a mental illness?

Did a possession make him capable of such grievous harm to himself?

Did the family know about it and that's why they had the sage ready to burn at the intervention?

Or if there wasn't a possession, could it be that his suicide was so violent his spirit can't move on?

Or was the moment so emotionally charged that the negative energy created by his violent death, somehow burned an image track of it into the rooms of that house?

I don't know the answer to these questions. All I know for sure is that unthinkable emotional and physical violence occurred in that place, and there has been something going on in it ever since, something unexplainable.

THE FACELESS MANNEQUIN
By Kevin Faulk

Being out and about at 3 a.m. is always a little unsettling, regardless of what you're doing. Writer Bram Stoker wrote: "No man knows till he has suffered from the night how sweet and dear to his heart and eye the morning can be." What makes this worse is working at an Oregon college that dates to the 1800's. Some of the buildings are old and creaky, many of them built over a pioneer cemetery.

It was part of my job description as a public safety officer to check the buildings to ensure there was no errant student or a non-student inside causing mischief.

On the night in question, I was making my rounds through all the structures when I came to a building that always pushed my needle deep into the red on the spine-tingling scale. It was the theater building, purchased by the university during World War II.

I'm convinced there is something fundamentally not normal about all theater buildings. Google lists lots of links to haunted theaters throughout the world. Hollywood, California, of course, boasts many haunted ones, to include the tourist-popular Mann's Chinese Theater. That one tops every theater list.

There were lots of things inside the old campus theater that toyed with one's imagination: its single nightlight that casts a "ghostly light" across its well-trodden stage; dressing room mirrors that never failed to scare the crap out of me when my reflection suddenly loomed in my flashlight beam; the basement with its metal operating table and a chair with binding straps on its arms (which all the officers jokingly *assumed* were props; and a particular area in one of the hallways that would give me chills every single time I passed through it.

Creepy, yes, but mostly explainable. But there were other things the officers, and many students and faculty could not explain. In fact, previous experiences I had had within the building encouraged my baser instincts to avoid the place altogether. One night, I didn't listen to them—though I should have.

I was making my way through the theater building when I passed by a door I had never opened. There was no reason to since the sign next to it indicated the room was for storage.

But this time I was curious.

I unlocked the padlock, turned the old knob, and pushed open the door to darkness. I clicked on my flashlight, and the beam fell on a black, faceless mannequin smack in the center of the room.

I forced a nervous laugh, took a few deep breaths to regain control of my heartbeat, and marveled at how one's mind can play games with—

The mannequin began rotating on its metal base toward me.

"You've got to be kidding me," I blurted into the strange room while scooting back out into the hall.

I stood motionless for a few moments staring at several old framed pictures adorning the hallway, though not actually seeing them. Then on a whim because, well, because sometimes I just do dumb things, I retrieved my iPhone and pushed the video button. I aimed it at the pictures for a second and then I slowly crept back into the darkness of the strange room.

I swept my flashlight to all four corners to ensure no one was in there and then settled the beam on the mannequin. If at this point I had fully believed it had actually moved, rather than it being a trick of the light beam or my imagination, which was admittedly heightened because of the theater's built-in creep factor, I would have exited the entire building with extreme haste.

I held my light on the featureless head for a moment, as it stood mute and motionless in the seldom used and always locked room. I smiled to myself and wondered how I could have thought a faceless, heartless, inanimate object that was only shaped like a human could ever move. I'm not one to take flights of fancy. I'm a veteran of the war in Afghanistan, a martial artist, and a father. It was ridiculous to think—

The mannequin moved again ... turning ever so slowly away from me.

My legs turned to mush, and I might have made an audible noise of some kind.

Somehow, I kept my phone's camera on the thing for a few more seconds. Then I wanted, no, I *had* to get out of there right that instant. I fast-walked—really, really fast-walked—to the nearest exit.

***

Looking back now, I sometimes wish I hadn't recorded it because then I could tell myself that my sleep-deprived eyes were deceiving me. But I know they weren't.

The mannequin moved, but how? Was it on a moving platform of some kind? If so, why wasn't it continuously rotating? And how would it have been powered? And if it were—in my gut I know it wasn't—why would it be powered at all since it was locked inside of a storeroom for I don't know how long?

Might a student have played a prank on a poor campus cop?

What an elaborate mission that would be. They would have to gain entry to the locked room somehow and then wait, and wait some more, never knowing if this would be the one time—the only time—I would look into the room or, for that matter, if I would even be checking the theater that night.

It was a very long time before I went into the room again and by then the mannequin had been moved to some other location.

Hell, maybe it moved there all by itself.

Editor's note: I saw the video, and it is indeed disturbingly creepy.

WHITE EAGLE
By Loren W. Christensen

Back in the late 1970s, there was an old tavern in my beat in Portland with a rich history of sordidness and violence. The place was a stone's throw from a railroad yard, and a second stone's throw from the mighty Willamette River. In the late 1800s through the first few decades of the 1900s, ship workers, railroad men, drifters, prostitutes, and criminals of every ilk kept things rootin' and tootin' and bleedin' in the place. Asian and black female prostitutes stayed in the basement, some against their will, and opium smokers shared a corner with them.

The 13 rooms on the second floor gave customers and prostitutes more privacy. A woman named Rose was murdered by a jealous brothel manager up there. Since then, people have reported smelling odors of wafting perfume, hearing a woman cry and other strange noises, and seeing a face at the upstairs window when not a living soul was on the second floor.

My partner Bill knew the manager, and we'd swing by occasionally to have coffee with him before he opened for business. He was sweeping the sidewalk in front of the pub the first time I met him, deep worry lines creasing his forehead.

"What's happenin', Dan?" Bill asked, after pulling us to the curb.

The two of them exchanged friendly digs for a minute before Dan asked us to come in for coffee.

The two-story structure was long and rectangular with empty lots on each side of it. There were other buildings next to it at one time, possibly attached, but the lots were vacant then, and they still are today.

There were only the three of us in the place that morning as we sat around a table next to a long bar. Chairs had been set upside down on all the other tables so that Dan, still looking as if something was bothering him, could clean the floor. We chatted for a while, and when I asked a question about the architecture, he frowned again and began fiddling mindlessly with a salt shaker.

"Sometimes in the morning," he said, his eyes still on the shaker, "the chairs aren't where I left them the night before."

We looked at him.

He looked a little uncomfortable as if he wished he could withdraw his words. He stood and reached for his broom where he left it propped against another table.

"Uh, you can't leave it at that, Dan," Bill said.

"No one works at night," he said, moving his broom around, though he had already swept the floor. "No cleaning crew. No anyone."

"Any sign of forced entry?" I asked.

He shook his head. "It's happened before too. Sometimes the chairs have been removed from the tops of the tables and sometimes they're all pushed into that far corner over there. One time they were scattered all about the floor."

***

McMenamins is a popular chain of over 65 pubs and hotels throughout Oregon and Washington. They buy old and unique buildings, schools, and hotels, add multiple themed pubs within a single sprawling complex, along with theaters and gift shops, and fill all available spaces with antique art. Several of their pubs and hotels have been declared haunted by paranormal investigators and written about in articles, books, and blogs. White Eagle is a relatively small pub McMenanins bought in 1993, but stories of things paranormal there are well known.

In recent years, psychics have reported feeling a powerful sense of violence and death in the basement area, and witnesses say they have seen floating brooms and mops. One employee felt hands push her down the stairs.

I perceived a weird vibe in the place those many years ago, a mild sense of something out-of-the-norm. Dan's story about moving furniture seemed fitting to what I was feeling.

I have been to the White Eagle a few times in the last few years, and while I had read about recent paranormal activity in the place, I didn't get that same vibe I did three decades ago. Maybe whatever it was is gone now.

Or maybe, as has happened in other haunted places, *it* is laying low for a while and will return on its schedule.

At night.

In the dark.

THE MAN IN THE WINDOW
By Jess Burlingham

"A house is never still in darkness to those who listen intently; there is a whispering in distant chambers, an unearthly hand presses the snib of the window, the latch rises." ~ J. M. Barrie

It was mid-October, halfway to All Hallows Eve and nearing midnight when dispatch sent Officer Nelson and me on a theft call to Greystone Lane in Richmond, Virginia. The old three-story house rested on a dead-end road, surrounded by a six-foot high chain-link fence. It was well-lit street, but the grounds around the house were in near darkness, no doubt making the thieves' job easier.

The owner met us outside and told us he was renovating the 100-year-old structure; at least he was before thieves ran off with his tools, metals, and an assortment of scrap materials from the grounds. He didn't know if anything had been taken from inside, although he had checked the doors and windows and didn't find any sign of entry.

Detective Roberts, a property crime detective, arrived and we began our investigation. We first checked the grounds on all four sides of the house, our flashlight beams penetrating every dark nook and cranny. We found nothing unusual. That is until I saw the figure in the upstairs window.

Actually, I felt it first, felt—him.

How? I'm not sure, other than I have always had a strong sixth sense about things. I know how that sounds, but it's true. This time I felt the hairs on the back of my neck stand on end an instant before I was drawn to the window.

The room behind the glass was dark but I could see well enough to know that whoever was looking out was male. Was he looking at me? At all of us? I couldn't tell, but it somehow felt to me that he knew I was connecting with him. I looked away to ask the owner if anyone was living in the house or if there were guests inside. He assured me there was no one.

When I looked back up, the figure was gone.

I informed Detective Roberts of what I had seen, and he told the owner that we needed to clear the inside for everyone's safety. (I think Detective Roberts thought I was a little crazy but in a few minutes he would be quite fearful.) The owner had no problem with this and remained outside as we slipped through the door. It took a while to search the place because there were three levels and lots of square footage but in the end, it was all clear. We asked the owner to come in and look around to see if anything was missing.

We followed him as he surveyed the place and all was fine. But when we began to ascend the stairs to the upper level—that's when we heard them.

Footsteps.

Coming from the top floor and in the direction of the window where I had the seen the man.

We all froze in place, except for the homeowner who acted as if he hadn't noticed anything unusual. When we told him what we had heard, he didn't seem surprised. I asked, half joking and half serious if the house might be haunted.

"Yes, it is," he said, his voice unaffected, though goose bumps were popping out all over me. "I don't know who the man—the ghost—is, but I do know he's older and he stays on the upper level."

He said it so nonchalantly it was as if he were referring to a kind old gentleman tenant. Maybe he was.

Not just a little unnerved, I managed to tell him what I had seen in the window from outside.

"Oh yes," he said matter-of-factly. "I'm not surprised. Others have seen the exact same thing up there."

STRANGE PLACE
By Loren W. Christensen

I wrote a chapter in Section Four called "Close Encounters of the Second Kind," which was about my experiences with UFOs on the edge of the Florida Everglades when I served there as a military policeman on an Army missile battery in the late 1960s. I encourage you to read that story first as it will make this one clearer.

As described in the "Close Encounters" piece, our headquarters' compound—offices, sleeping quarters, chow hall, and rec room—were a mile down the road from what we called "down range"—a larger area that contained three huge missile barns, the dog kennels, an assortment of trailers and smaller buildings, and a ranch-style house where men could eat, sleep, and watch TV. For some unknown reason, my perceptions of the strangeness of the place never occurred in the headquarters' area but only down range. There my acuities were rich indeed.

As an MP dog handler, I worked at night. There were eight of us and we generally worked four-man/dog teams per shift and patrolled the outer perimeter of the grounds in pairs, though at times we went out alone. The 10-acres was carved out of the jungle, a terrible place densely populated with uncountable insects, slithering critters, little hairy animals, and 'gators with wide, yawning jaws. Not a place for a city boy like me.

There were three other missile batteries in the Everglades, and we would occasionally hear about one of them experiencing what paranormal investigators call a "full apparition." As the name implies, this is a sighting of a complete or partial body of a ghost or spirit, which typically fades away as soon as someone sees it. The MPs at the other missile batteries reported seeing only the top half of an apparition, a woman. They said as soon as they shined their flashlights on it or turned on their vehicle headlights, the image dissolved. I never witnessed it, but it was a constant story batted around during my year stationed in Florida.

The experiences at my battery were more about what we sensed and, on one occasion, how my dog acted, or rather, reacted.

To something unseen.

When we weren't out patrolling, we hung out in a small brick blockhouse that was used during the day to sign people in before entering the missile area. But at night, we often took cover there from the hordes of mosquitos, and we would shoot the breeze until it was our turn to patrol the perimeter. We would then walk about 100 yards to the kennels, retrieve our dogs, and head out. But sometimes that short walk through the thick darkness was fear-provoking, especially strange because there was no tangible reason for it.

The feeling—and to reiterate it didn't happen every time to me—was a combination of feeling watched, anxiety, hypervigilance, goose-pimpled flesh, dread, and of intense anticipation. But why?

Because I was a big tough soldier who worked with attack dogs, I didn't share my feelings with any of the guys because the ridicule would have been of biblical proportions. Or so I thought.

One night three other MPs and I were in the brick blockhouse talking about whatever young soldiers gab about when I commented about the spooky walk to the kennels. The room suddenly became quiet and all eyes were on me. One second passed … two … Then they all began talking at once.

"I knoooow."

"I hate that walk."

"Walk? I run."

"I always keep my hand on my gun."

No one had an explanation, but all felt the same strange atmosphere and found it frightening.

Fritz, my 70-pound German shepherd, was trained to alert on people and discouraged to alert on animals. That was the idea, anyway. But eons of hunting for food are hard to drill out of a dog in eight weeks of training. When Fritz would alert on a human in the dark, he would lift his head high. If it were very dark out, I would bend down and look between his ears to detect the person he had spotted silhouetted against the sky. When he would forget his training and alert on an animal or snake, he would duck his head nearly to the ground.

The long stretch of dark double-fenced area often gave me the creeps even when I was with Fritz, who was tough enough to shred the face from a bronze statue. One night the feeling was particularly intense as we patrolled alone on the backside of the compound. The darkness was dense with visibility no more than a few feet in any direction.

Fritz stopped. He didn't lift his head or lower it, growl or bark, or give me any other kind of warning as he had done a hundred times before.

Instead, he sprang off the ground and slammed into my chest with all four feet.

I fell onto my back, and because the leash was attached to my wrist, Fritz nearly ripped my arm out of my shoulder socket as he tried to yank himself free to bolt in the opposite direction.

I outweighed him by 120 pounds, but that didn't keep him from trying to drag me. I shouted "No!" repeatedly, as I pulled on the cyclone fence to get to my feet. Even after I had gotten up, Fritz continued his struggle to get away. Somehow, I managed to retrieve my flashlight from my belt clip and point a beam into the dark.

There was nothing there. Even the swamp outside the fence was still.

No way was I going to continue in that direction, even if Fritz would have let me, which he wouldn't have. We half walked, and half ran back to the corner, hung a right turn, and hurried along the width of the compound to the kennel shack. Only then did the feeling of being watched and … followed, dissipate.

It took a while before Fritz relaxed and was his usual cheerful attack-dog self. It took me a little longer, plus my chest hurt where he hit me.

***

Eight years later, I was out of the service and on vacation with a long layover at Miami International Airport. To kill time, I rented a car and drove out to the Keys and up the narrow, winding road to the missile battery. The headquarters was still fenced in but gone was the sharp military look of the place. Now windows were broken, exterior paint was flaking off, and weeds were everywhere. I drove on to where the missiles had been kept and found that area in the same condition. I got out of the car and walked over to the cyclone fence to get a closer look, which immediately drew the attention of two MPs.

I told them I had been stationed there for a year and wanted to check it out. They said I was just in time because it was going to be torn down the very next day. They also told me I couldn't come inside the fence.

It was strange seeing it again and knowing it would soon be gone. Besides the experiences I've told here and in the chapter, "Close Encounters of the Second Kind," I also had non paranormal experiences that profoundly affected me.

I started to leave but decided, what the heck. I told the MPs a little about the UFOs and the general creepiness of the place, and asked if they had experienced anything similar. They both nodded vigorously.

"Ooooh, yeah," one of them said. "I'll be glad to get out of this place. It's weird here."

"Very weird," the other man concurred.

I understood them wanting to leave. The UFOs were the final straw for me when I served in the battery. I decided I could deal with the Vietcong, but this strange place was just too much.

I went into the First Sergeant's office and volunteered to go to the war.

FOREST LAWN CEMETERY
By Steven R. Alva

In 1983, I was a young police officer finishing out my probationary period in Hollywood Division. The violence in Hollywood back then was such that you could go out for breakfast and have a busboy run up to your table to say he just found dismembered body parts inside a dumpster out back. There were a constant plethora of runaway kids that came from all over the country "to be discovered," only to become street urchins on Hollywood Boulevard, and then eventually disappear never to be heard from again.

If you drove from east to west on the famous street, you would see groups of female prostitutes standing on every corner and sellers of narcotics offering everything from heroin to hashish to speed. Santa Monica Boulevard wasn't any better, with male prostitutes strolling the street cruising for customers. Overseeing this circus from high up in the hills were the very rich and very famous.

It was a fast-paced division, and I learned much from the senior officers, many of whom worked those streets all their careers. The experience made for some excellent cops with highly developed street smarts and intuition. I have always felt lucky I was able to work with them.

As crazy as this atmosphere was, one night we got a radio call we would never forget.

It was around 3:30 a.m., and my partner and I were working 6Adam15 when dispatch gave us a code-30 audible at Forest Lawn Cemetery. There were listening devices inside the main building, and the alarm company could hear talking and banging inside the place.

Forest Lawn Cemetery is located on the very edge of Hollywood Division, next to Studio City. The lighting was poor on the private street leading into the cemetery, causing many bad traffic accidents.

We turned off our lights as we approached so we didn't give away our arrival. We parked a short distance away from the building and began moving toward it on foot. We proceeded slowly, visually clearing the grounds of anyone hiding or waiting for us, a task made difficult since the cemetery grounds were unlit. But why would they put lights in a cemetery, anyway?

The building in question looked to be an old, two-story American colonial structure. I would learn later that the bottom floor was a chapel, and the second floor contained a display room and a prep area where the dead were dressed and made up before laid out in their coffins.

Another two-man unit arrived to cover us, and quickly positioned themselves by the front door while my partner and I checked the building's perimeter looking for signs of forced entry. We didn't find any.

Dispatch: *"6Adam15, be advised the alarm company can hear loud talking inside the location right now."*

"We're outside of it," I replied, "It appears to be locked. Have security meet us here with the keys."

No sooner had I said that than a security officer appeared out of the darkness, his eyes large with ... fear? I told him we had received a radio call of a possible burglary with noises heard inside the structure. When I said that we would like to go in and clear the place of suspects or see if there was indeed a crime committed, he thrust the keys at me instead of opening the door for us. I must have looked surprised because he said something that I didn't understand—but I would in a few minutes.

"I don't come up here after dark," he said, his eyes even larger than before. "And never to this building."

We slipped through the door, two teams at a time, one covering the other as we cleared rooms, one by one, continually assessing for threats as we moved. Ninety percent of alarm calls are false, so I was beginning to think this was just another one set off by the wind or a cat. But it wasn't windy and—

A loud bang from the stairwell followed by heavy footsteps running up to the second floor.

The stairs were the only escape route from up there, and we moved toward them together, weapons drawn; one of the officers told dispatch to send us a dog unit because we had a burglar confined. We covered the bottom of the stairs and waited.

Loud banging.

This time from all the way up the stairs, and it sounded as if someone were throwing things on the floor or against the walls.

We held our position until the K9 unit arrived. We told the officer we believed we had a burglary suspect cornered on the second level, and we wanted him to send his dog up the stairs to search. Police K9 dogs really love the action. Give them a suspect to chase, and they are in doggy heaven. Tell them to watch a prone suspect, and they are happier than when given a T-bone steak. Tell them to run up a set of stairs to nab a bad guy …

The dog refused to go into the building.

The handler insisted. "Go get 'em, boy!" he encouraged. "Get the bad guy! That's my baby, go get the bad guy!" The handler unleashed him. "Go get the—"

The dog spun about and ran madly away into the cemetery in the opposite direction, his handler in pursuit, shouting for him to come back.

From upstairs, a radio blared to life.

Enough. It was time to get this guy. Halfway up the stairs the lights snapped on, and we all reflexively crouched. Any doubt we had before about anyone being up there was gone. It had to be someone moving around and—

The lights went off, as did the radio.

We hesitated for a moment and then continued our stealthy climb. The second level room was full of caskets. My skin crawled at the thought of having to search for someone hiding in them. But it had to be done. With my weapon in hand, I commenced moving across the floor, my flashlight beam penetrating the darkness and—

A metal gurney lay on its side in total disarray. Did this make the noise the alarm company heard? A portable radio sat on a nearby desk. The hair on the back of my neck stiffened as my light moved over the source of the banging and the source of the music, both now still and silent. But there was no one up there.

Confident the second floor was clear, we began filing back down the stairs. Then the music came on again. I spun about and looked back up into the darkness. The music went silent.

There was not a living soul up there. We just looked.

Outside, the security guard was waiting by my patrol car. I returned the building keys to him without uttering a word, and he took them from me without speaking. I radioed dispatch that everything was secure and there was no evidence of a burglary. I exhaled a long calming breath and began to open my car door when a light caught my eye.

It was coming from the second story window.

HAUNTED PLACES IN THE NEWS

Eastern State Penitentiary
The Pennsylvania Prison System controlled Eastern State from 1829 to 1913. While the systems were used by the Quakers as a place for prisoners to look inside themselves and find God, the solitude drove many men, otherwise perfectly sane, to total madness. The place was notorious for its torture devices, though the Quakers denied any involvement.

The Hole, a pit dug under a cellblock, was a hellish place where rule-breakers were confined for weeks at a time with only bread and water to keep them barely alive.

Inmates who disobeyed the prison's communication rules suffered the Iron Gag, a terrible device that was clamped onto the prisoner's tongue then linked to his wrists that were wrenched up behind him. The slightest movement tore the prisoner's tongue. The device took the lives of many people.

The Bath was a method of punishment in which an inmate was submerged in ice-cold water and then hung on a wall all night. During the winter, it was common for a layer of ice to form over the inmate by morning.

There were far worse punishments than these. Add to that the overcrowding issue. Although the prison was designed for 250 inmates, over 1700 of them jammed the hell hole before it closed in 1913.

Not surprisingly, the old structure is a hotbed for paranormal activity. Here are two.

A locksmith was working on a 140-year-old cellblock lock when a force of some kind suddenly prevented him from moving. He reported seeing anguished faces on the cell walls, and he felt a powerful draw to the negative energy that many paranormal investigators say he unleashed by releasing the old lock.

Tourists and employees often report hearing giggling, whispering, and crying.

Over two dozen investigations are conducted a year in the prison, and nearly every time the teams find evidence of paranormal activity.

Source: *About News*

*

West Virginia Penitentiary

A worker reported that an invisible force physically stopped him from entering an area known as the Sugar Shack.

"I had my arms full of tools, and I was about halfway through the room when I felt pressure on my shoulder. It was as if someone placed their hand on it and stopped me. I definitely know there is some kind of activity here."

Another worker opened a door into a cellblock and could hear what sounded like someone kicking a cell door. "It echoed through the whole room. I've heard EVPs here, but nothing scared me like that time."

A tour guide began his job as a skeptic, but his experiences quickly made him a believer. "The place is very creepy and you never know when you're going to see something. I've seen figures in different places right when I was giving a tour. Visitors report hearing and seeing things too."

Source: *Discovery*

*

Alcatraz

Two tourists were spooked after they took a photograph in the prison's visitation center. The photo depicts what appears to be a young woman looking into the camera from inside the prison's visitation area.

The photographer, a teaching assistant from the UK, said, "As soon as we entered the prison, everything felt eerie. I didn't feel comfortable there. While I was doing an audio-tour of the place, I casually snapped the empty visitation block window. When I glanced at the picture on my phone, I saw this dark female figure in the picture. I looked at the window again, and there was no one in the room."

Source: *Daily Mail, UK*

*

Licking County Jail, Ohio

Constructed in 1889 and closed several decades ago, there appear to be prisoners still "locked up" in the old structure that some people in Newark consider an eyesore.

Southeastern Ohio Paranormal Investigators spent a chilly night in the old jail in November of 2011. They brought with them an assortment of high-tech tools that enabled them to capture EVPs and an apparition that appeared to be looking out from a basement room.

The two lead investigators, Tom Robinson and Michelle Duke, are corrections officers with the Zanesville Police Department and have over 30 combined years of experience in paranormal investigations.

The two played their recordings and talked about their findings with people from the community and the county. Those in favor of tearing the old structure down are now concerned after the sudden interest in the place. They are worried that Robinson and Duke's investigation, as well as other reports of hauntings at the site, might save the old jail.

Source: *The Columbus Dispatch,* Ohio

*

Chatham County Jail

The Savannah (Georgia) Ghost Research team spent a night in the old jail in 2015 and captured 50 recordings, some more clear than others, which is almost always the case. Ryan Dunn, the man in charge of the investigative team, said they got several direct responses to questions asked by the group.

At one point, Dunn asked if there were a presence with them to knock three times. The recording picked up three knocks.

When one of their devices buzzed during the investigation, a recorded voice can be heard to ask, "Was that an alarm?"

Dunn said, "We caught this shadow figure on a thermal camera that was walking back and forth in the halls. [An investigator] got a photo of it on thermal, and we saw it come into one of the cells, crouch down, stand up, and walk right back out. It was a little unsettling."

Source: *Fox 10 TV*

Pentridge Prison, Australia

There is a frequently seen apparition at the now-closed Pentridge Prison that looks like one of its former notorious inmates, a man who went by Chopper Read. Many night visitors passing through the area known as D-Division have seen the figure.

Sometimes the shadow watches them as it leans against the wall outside his cell, Cell-16. Other times, people see the shadow lighting a cigarette before moving into the cell.

Jeremy Kewley, a tour guide at the prison, was taking a group around one night in the summer of 2014. He prefaced his story by saying that the prison in general "is quite eerie, to say the least." At one point during that tour, Kewley led his group to the end of a block of cells.

"Suddenly," Kewley says, "from Cell-16, a male voice loudly and aggressively shouted, 'GET OUUUUUT!' It was very scary and we all jumped. Then we moved away quite quickly. We called the police. Can you believe it? The police were called because that was just not right."

Officers came and thoroughly searched the block and the cells, but they didn't find anything.

During his incarceration, Chopper was allowed outside of his small cell to walk about the larger caged area. He would lean against the wall, smoke cigarettes, and watch other inmates roam the corridors.

Chopper Read died in 2013.

Source: *Herald Sun*

Indiana

People in Gary, including the local police captain, believe that several ghosts and demons haunt a house on an otherwise quiet street. The location has generated many police reports of strange occurrences over the years.

One family fled because of the sheer volume of paranormal events, to include children levitated, sounds of footsteps, and odd behavior by animals and insects.

Psychics informed the family that there are over 200 ghosts and demons in the place and it appears they are trying to possess the three children.

At one point, a family physician diagnosed the complaints as hallucinations, but only at first. Medical staff at the physician's office witnessed one of the children being lifted and thrown against the wall without anyone touching him.

The family moved, and the new occupants have not experienced anything unusual. However, the police captain who visited the family before they moved out said he was now "a believer" in ghosts and demons.

Source: *Huffington Post* and *Examiner.com*

*

Texas

"Some officers would rather not go upstairs by themselves at night," said one from the Richmond, Texas Police Department. "In fact, it's so spooky an officer has given tours of the station for 12 years."

"We've heard people, sounds like little kids running upstairs, but there is no one up there," said a dispatcher. Most recently, she heard a voice on the intercom say, "Get out!" No one else was in the building at the time.

The Richmond Police station was built in 1897 and served as the county jail. The sheriff and his family lived on the ground floor, black inmates stayed in the basement, and Hispanics upstairs. Gallows still stand in the police station where the condemned hung by their neck until dead.

A medium—without any prior information—froze in her tracks in the basement. Staring at a back wall, she said, "I'm getting an image of somebody being hacked and beaten."

An officer said that is exactly what used to happen on that wall.

Source: *KHOU TV*

*

Pittsburg

The Greater Pittsburg Paranormal Society recently offered audio and video evidence that something is going on inside the Homestead Police Department. The evidence has vindicated staffers at the station who have long reported the sounds of doors slamming and of footsteps, and the occasional taps on the shoulder.

During a meeting, an electric typewriter turned itself on and started typing. Another time a broken sidewalk cleaner turned on without a key. Similar reports reached a stage where the police chief allowed the Paranormal Society to come in and investigate.

The investigators picked up the sound of a scream in the basement, the sound of a door slamming in the attic, and a loud voice booming, "Hey Sam," followed by another door slamming.

A video showed a video camera cord, which they had taped to the ceiling, being pulled loose. "It didn't simply fall," the investigator said. "It's like someone pulled it loose."

Another video showed a shadow moving behind a window, the same window where officers have reported feeling watched as they pass.

One investigator reported that when she was in the attic, an invisible entity tapped on her shoulder and pulled her hair upward.

The lead paranormal investigator says the haunting is residual, meaning it's not interactive with people who work there.

Then how does that explain the touching and hair pulling?

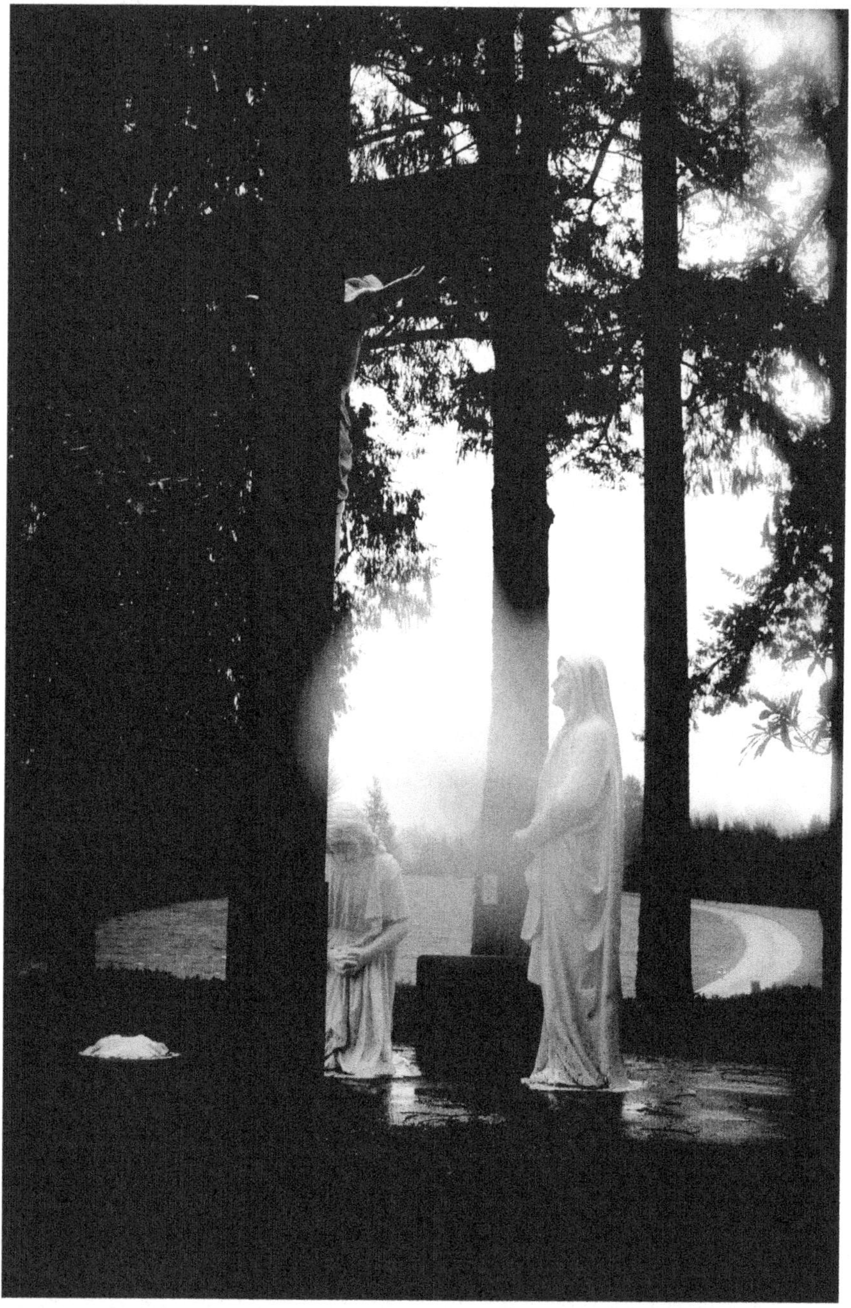

SECTION THREE

DIVINE INTERVENION AND DEMONS

Divine intervention is a gift from a higher realm of existence: the Biblical God, the Creator, the Buddha, or what many call a Higher Power.

Divine intervention is a guardian that redirects us to prevent something from happening or redirects us to a place where we can help someone or experience something of value.

A demon is a persistently tormenting person or supernatural force.

A demon is a supernatural, often malevolent being prevalent in religion, occultism, literature, fiction, mythology, and folklore.

SCRATCHES
By Rich Perez

I've been on the Houston Police Department for nearly 23 years, and I've served in the US Navy, both active and reserves, for almost 29. I've done two tours in the Iraq War, the last one working with the Army.

I didn't begin believing in God and the supernatural until after some things happened in my middle teens—good and not so good—that I couldn't explain. As a realist, I searched for answers to what these occurrences meant, and I found a connection with the spiritual side that blew me away. It allowed me to not fear death, and it compelled me to always listen to that benevolent "inner voice." It has not only saved my life on the job, but "the voice" made decisions I would not have made before it entered my life.

I've also had experiences with what I believe to have been "unseen assailants." On three occasions, beginning in 2009, I was repeatedly injured by what I conclude to be some type of malevolent spirit. I can't validate this because I've never felt the assaults as they happened; I discovered the injuries—long scratches on my body—afterwards.

I did, however, find a pattern to them.

Each one happened on a domestic disturbance call with a highly dysfunctional family unit of three to five members. Each occurred in an apartment in disarray, with blinds closed, and lights dimmed on bright, sunny Texas days.

I always try to do what feels right on family disturbance calls. Sometimes it's just a talk. Other times it's an arrest of one or more participants. My third option is to arbitrate with a positive spiritual spin. Before leaving a family, I typically say, "Open up the blinds and let some of God's light in. It's free."

The first time I got home after handling a domestic disturbance call during my shift, I began peeling off my gun belt, shirt, and vest, as was my routine. But before I could completely remove my vest, I felt a burning pain in my back. When I pulled off my T-shirt, my wife jokingly asked, "Who have you been sleeping with?" I told her nobody, today. She laughed and said there were scratches on my back.

When I looked in the mirror, I found two long, thin scratches running diagonally from my right shoulder to just above my left hip. I figured my vest somehow scratched me through my T-shirt, but that didn't make sense because the shirt is worn to protect the skin. That first time was five years ago after I had returned from serving in the Middle East.

About a year later, I went to another family fight that had the same elements as the one just described: a small apartment, dimly lit, and a dysfunctional family. I did my best to patch things up with my usual constructive intervention with a spiritual twist. I came home, peeled off my uniform and felt that same burning sensation on my back as I had a year earlier.

This time, I discovered three thin marks, also diagonal, but running in the opposite direction, from my lower left shoulder to my right hip. The middle scratch was longer than those on each side of it.

The last time I experienced this was in 2014. I went to another family fight in an apartment, same closed curtains, dim lighting on a sunny day, and another dysfunctional family. I gave my usual lecture, but this time I took one of the family members to jail on a warrant.

I went home, stripped off my gear, and when I removed my vest, I once again felt that same burning.

This time I found two horizontal scratches across on my back.

I've handled many domestic disturbance calls on the job, but these three all had the same elements.

I've shared my stories with a few officers, but not one of them has experienced the same thing.

A SIGN IN TWISTED METAL
By Ryan Schwoebel

I grew up in a household that was "quasi-Christian," meaning we attended church sporadically and on major holidays. I got involved in Christian youth groups in middle school, eventually becoming born again. But over time, especially in my college years, I walked away from my Christian faith.

In part, this was due to the partying lifestyle in my fraternity, as well as my exposure to agnostic and atheistic viewpoints from my professors. I was a psychology major, and this was my first exposure to lines of thinking that were rational, that used deductive logic, and that didn't allow for superstition and religious interpretations to prevail over peer-reviewed, scientific methods.

When I was a boy, I longed to be a cop. My mom tells of washing my clothes and continually finding holes in my shirts where I had worn a toy badge. As I got older, thoughts of a career in law enforcement waned, particularly in my teen years.

That changed as I was beginning my junior year in college, still without a real focus on what I wanted to do after graduation. But when those planes slammed into the Twin Towers on September 11, 2001, I decided law enforcement was what I wanted to pursue. I brought my grades up from C's and D's to A's and B's and pursued internships with police agencies.

While working my first job out of college, I decided to join my local sheriff's office—Jefferson County, Alabama—as a sworn reserve deputy sheriff. I wasn't state certified so I could only ride on patrol with a deputy who was.

Wanting to gain as much practical experience as I could, I went out every weekend on patrol for eight-hour shifts. The certified deputy usually drove, and I was the eager rookie riding shotgun.

About two years into this routine, one of my regular partners called to inform me that something came up at his full-time job, so he wouldn't be able to go out on patrol that night. If he couldn't go out I couldn't go out either, so I made other plans for the weekend.

A couple of days later, I learned that the deputy had managed to get off work in time to go on patrol, but figuring I was already busy he didn't call me. Shortly after his shift began, a car T-boned his patrol unit, completely crushing in the passenger side where I always sat.

The unhurt deputy later told me, "I'm so glad you didn't come out with me. You would most certainly have been killed if you had been sitting in that seat."

I had been praying over the last few months for God to show me a sign that He was real. I asked Him, in His own way and in His own time, to reveal Himself in a manner that spoke directly to me, so I would know for sure.

This experience changed my life, and it's part of the reason that today I teach 7th and 8th grade Sunday school at my church.

THE VOICE
By Greg Kade

"God puts people in our paths for certain reasons." ~ Greg Kade

July 3, 2006
I've been working for the Raleigh County Sheriff's Department in West Virginia since 2002.

On the night of the shooting in 2006, I was technically off duty and working a security job at a construction site. Deputy Hajash, the newest member of the department, stopped by for a short visit. A moment later he got a radio call on a man standing in the middle of the street firing a gun at his own house.

I could see the concern on the deputy's face—he was quite young, and there was no available backup—so I logged on duty with dispatch, told Hajash to lead the way, and I would gather additional information as I followed in my own vehicle. Dispatch told me there were two young girls in the home with their mother, and it was their father who was shooting at the house with a handgun.

When we got close to the scene, I told the young officer to pull over so we would approach on foot.

"Are you taking anything?" Hajash asked, which is cop-speak for: "Are you taking a long gun?"

"No," I said, and began to head out. But I had taken no more than 10 steps when a booming voice spoke to me.

Take your shotgun!

It sent chills to my very core. I don't know if God allowed my deceased father to tell me this or if it came from God himself, but I know for sure that the loud-and-clear warning, the command, came only to me.

So, I returned to my car and retrieved my Remington 870 shotgun with tac light. My AR15 was out for service.

As we neared the house, we didn't hear gunfire but rather loud music, which dispatch confirmed was coming from the suspect's pickup. The home was located toward the back of the property with a large yard on one side. We stopped near its corner and spotted a male walking in and out of shadows made by a dusk-to-dawn light attached over the garage.

I instructed Hajash that we would proceed down the fence, go through the gate, and I'd split right, and he would go left. The idea was to get into a position between the man and the house. But as luck would have it, the gate was locked. The music was quite loud now, so I told Hajash that we would climb the fence and move around the corners of the house. I handed my shotgun to him and began to scoot. But just as I was halfway up, the music stopped.

"What the hell!" It was the man. For a moment I thought he might have seen me but he was actually referring to the music suddenly stopping.

Hajash and I could not get the rest of the way over the fence without making noise, so I gently climbed back down. I whispered that it would be better to go around the corner, approach the gunman from the road, and try to prevent him from fleeing toward the house. Fortunately, an eight-foot-high hedgerow hid our advance.

When I saw the tailgate of a full-sized pickup, I switched on my weapon light and began to sidestep to engage the man. I could see him leaning in his open door, incongruously wearing only Tighty-Whitie under briefs.

"Police!" I shouted. "Show me your hands!"

Dispatch told us he had a handgun, but when he turned toward us, he was shouldering an AK47 and lifting it in our direction.

I squeezed my trigger.

Most my 00 buckshot went into the suspect's weapon but the rest punched through his head. He dropped.

The mind distorts perceptions at such times. My hearing blocked out Hajash's shots and mine, but the sound of the AK47 hitting the concrete driveway sounded like an explosion. I shouted at Hajash to take cover and watch the house.

A few months earlier I had served a court order at a private residence. A moment later, family members from five other houses on the same street came to interfere. The situation became volatile, but we managed to serve that warrant successfully. I was concerned something similar might happen this time, and I was particularly concerned the young girls would come out and see their dead father. Fortunately, backup arrived, and further problems were avoided.

I truly believe God was watching out for us during this tragic incident.

The first time was when we were approaching the house in our vehicles. If we had taken the shortest driving route instead of the one driven by Hajash, we would have driven to the side of the house where the shooter was and where there was no cover or concealment. The gunman would have had a superior advantage in the gunfight because of his elevated position and line of sight.

Second, when Hajash and I were approaching the pickup, we waded through nearly three dozen pieces of spent brass from when the gunman had been shooting at his house. With God's help, we walked right through all those shell casings without kicking any aside with our feet. If we had, we would have given away our position, and the gunman might very well have shot us first.

Thirdly, Hajash's was a fine police officer, but his shooting skills weren't his strongest asset. Although I feel like we helped each other get through the ordeal, some officers, including non-religious ones, as well as Hajash's mother, believe I was put into the situation to get him through it safely.

July 3, 2007, exactly one year later

I had sought counseling in the months after the shooting because no matter how justified, taking a life is difficult. Making it even worse was that I could relate to the man being a father. I had a young daughter, as well, and I had just found out I had another on the way. My utmost concern from the moment I squeezed my trigger was for the man's daughters.

On July 3, one year to the day since the shooting, I was a corporal working the night shift. Although I was still having issues with what happened a year earlier, I knew if I didn't go in I would never be able to work another July 3rd and 4th. My wife was at home listening to a police scanner, which I had never allowed in the house, but she understood how important the date was to my psyche, and had gotten one from somewhere.

Within two minutes of my shooting 12 months earlier, dispatch put out a call on an armed man barricaded inside his house and holding his family hostage.

He had already discharged a shotgun inside the home.

My wife called me within seconds, upset and talking a mile a minute. She didn't want me to go to the call. Let the others handle it, she pleaded. You don't have to go this time.

"Melissa," I said affectionately. "What kind of a man would I be if I didn't go?" With that she knew I was taking the call.

I always pray anytime I get a hot call or execute a high-risk search warrant. On the way to the barricaded armed man, I prayed, "Dear Heavenly Father, please keep us all safe and let this end without violence. But should the need for violence arise, please let us all go back home to our families. And God, if it's my time, please take care of my family and always let them remember I loved them."

We took up our tactical positions at the scene, and I used my cruiser's PA system to talk the guy into giving up. He came out peacefully five minutes later.

But I know in my heart that it wasn't me who got through to the distraught man. It was God using me to get him to turn himself over to law enforcement. That Sunday, I told my pastor what happened. He smiled gently, and said, "Greg, don't you see. God has healed you. Your internal strife should be over."

Yes, most of my personal conflict was over, and it was made abundantly clear by the way the call regarding the barricaded man played out. But there was one thing that continued to hover over my head: I knew that one day I would meet the daughters of the man I killed.

This year I did.

As a school resource officer now, a teacher contacted me to say one of the daughters wanted to meet me. Was I nervous? Oh yes, more than I ever was during my 28 boxing matches. The emotions were running high, as one of these young ladies was sitting on the tailgate of my pickup truck needing to know what happened that night. My wife told the girl, in a gentle, motherly tone, that it had been a horrific experience for me too, and that I had sought professional help. That softened the mood and made it a little easier to tell her what had happened. It was important that she actually hear, not just listen to my explanation of that night.

It was clear that my side of the story, which conflicted with the skewed version her family had told her, confused the young lady. In the end, she said she wanted to get to know us, and with that, the seed of communication had been planted, and it's now beginning to grow.

***

I used to ask myself why God would let this happen to me. I believe now that it all comes back to what I said earlier: God puts people in our paths for specific reasons.

Whenever I relate my story to someone, I get emotional telling about the Voice that spoke to me so loud and clear that night. I'll go to my grave knowing it was from above.

HE PULLED THE TRIGGER FOUR TIMES
By Loren W. Christensen

You got to be tough to live out West and never was that expression more true than on that December day when freezing rain was pinging off the roof of the police car, and a howling wind had dropped the wind chill to 15 degrees below zero.

Veteran Officer Jace Lansford patrolled the streets of his beat as usual, though he didn't expect much to happen on such a miserable and bitterly cold day. But he was about to get a call from dispatch that would heat things up and change his life forever, as well as the life of another man.

"Complainant says she was taking a shower," dispatch said, *"and a man began chopping through the outside wall of her house, just on the other side of her shower stall."*

Officer Lansford got there as quick as he could on the dangerous streets, but the suspect was gone. Neighbors who had heard the commotion met the officer out in the ice rain and said the man was rambling incoherently and appeared high. The officer took the complainant's information then parked a block away to write up the report and watch the streets.

Lansford had yet to go back into service when another beat car was dispatched to a residential alarm in his district. He grabbed the mic and told radio he would take the call but asked for the other car to keep coming. There are lots of alarms on stormy days; this time he had a feeling, and the veteran officer always trusted his gut.

Lansford got there first. He slid over a fence and found the backdoor to the home damaged. His gut feeling intensified, and he decided it was best to wait for his backup. But the second officer couldn't get over the fence, so he told Lansford he would get a shotgun and come around the other side.

He had no longer left when the burglar came out the back door and froze in place when he saw the uniformed officer standing a few feet away.

The burglar, William Warren, was high and his mind was dulled and foggy. This wasn't the 26-year-old's first face-to-face with a police officer; in fact, beginning as a child there had many, and none of them had been pleasant for the man who had a long history of drugs, burglaries, car theft, fights, and possession of stolen firearms.

Warren had lived for years with his mother in one of the city's crime-infested projects; getting pinched by the police was just part of his life. Warren was just a teenager when his father, far from an upright citizen, introduced the boy to cross tops and crank, which started the lad on a 20-year love affair with hard drugs.

"I had no fear," Warren said, "because I was seeing everything through a big fog. After getting scared away from the first house, I went to another but they had a big dog. I kicked in the door anyway, which set off a loud alarm. I was stoned, and I went in regardless. I was busy collecting stuff when I saw the police car pull up outside."

Officer Lansford drew his gun and shouted at the man that had just exited the house to put up his hands. "But he kept moving closer to me," Lansford said. "I backed up, keeping my gun on him. He kept coming until he was about four feet away. He was making arm movements as if trying to distract me. He wanted to lunge for my gun."

Lansford sighted his weapon on the man and shouted commands, but the burglar casually turned and began walking away.

Lansford didn't see him pull a gun. He would say later that it was as if Warren suddenly had it in his hand when he turned around. It was a cheap, Saturday night special.

"I just wanted to scare the cop away," Warren says. But that's not what happened.

Gunfire.

Warren's gun was pointed at Lansford's chest as he squeezed the trigger once, twice, three times, and then a fourth.

Lansford says, "It was as if I was outside my body watching myself fire my gun."

His first round punched through Warren's side and went out his back. The next one went through the man's stomach and crushed his spine.

Warren remembers, "I instantly felt all the electricity leave my lower body."

Lansford took cover behind the corner of the house. He could hear Warren cursing and saying over and over, "I wasn't going to shoot you."

When the two officers finally rounded the corner, their guns pointing, they saw Warren scooting on his rear and dragging his dead legs. "I'm paralyzed!" he shouted over and over. "I'm paralyzed! I wasn't going to shoot you."

He certainly tried. Four times. But his gun hadn't fired. The hammer dented the primer of four cartridges, but not one exploded out the end of the barrel that was pointed dead center on Lansford's chest.

Warren would be in and out of the hospital for several months. Finally, when he was well enough to go to court, the judge gave the man only five years of probation. Not one day behind bars for attempting to kill a police officer.

Lansford was enraged because of the light sentence.

Warren was enraged because he had been shot.

In time, Lansford decided he couldn't stay angry forever, and he asked his church to pray for him and the burglar.

Warren had mellowed too. He said, "Why was I hating a guy for doing the same thing I would have done if the roles were reversed.

A year later, Lansford and his partner pulled over a car leaving a known drug house. Warren was inside. Officers drew down on him, searched him and the car, but they didn't find anything. Meanwhile, Warren's father, a career criminal, repeatedly made threats to kill Lansford, not just because of what happened to his son, but because Lansford had arrested him repeatedly on drug charges.

Over the next six years, Warren continued to hang out with his doper friends, all of whom idolized him for trying to kill a cop. At one point, he was arrested in California during a drug raid and sent back to his home state where he was sentenced to a year in prison for probation violation. Warren said it was a blessing because he got into a drug program behind bars and was clean when he got released.

Warren found a job and avoided his drug friends. More importantly, he pondered why his life had been spared. "In the hospital," he said, "I had an out-of-body-experience, and I could feel myself going toward God. But I had done so many bad things in my life that I was sent back to correct them."

Warren also heard that Lansford had asked his church to pray for him.

After the former burglar got a car equipped so he could drive, he would often cruise the country roads. One day he passed a sign for a Catholic church. "I couldn't see it from the road, but I got curious and drove down it to find a big, beautiful church. I was immediately drawn to it, but the doors were closed."

The next day he called the church and told them he wanted to become a Catholic. The church treated him warmly, but they said the process would take a year. A daunting task, Warren thought, but he decided to do it. He went to the classes, attended services, and a year later he was baptized a Catholic.

Lansford lost contact with Warren, but he never forgot the man who tried four times to shoot him. One day he ran into Warren's parole officer, and he learned the man had cleaned up his act and was living near Portland. So out of the blue, Officer Lansford called Warren's home. The time was right, he thought.

Warren's mother answered. Remarkably, she said her son had wanted to contact the officer too.

Warren said, "I had been wanting to go to the police station, but I was concerned the officers would think I was up to no good. So I decided I would write him a letter." But Officer Lansford called him before he could send it. "We were both uncomfortable," Warren said, "but we agreed to meet at a restaurant."

It was indeed strained at first. The two men debriefed the incident piece by piece, and it became a real healing moment for them. The second time they met, they hugged.

Subsequently, Warren and Lansford joined forces—the burglar and the cop—to talk to church youth groups about their experience. They talked about Warren's long life of crime, the shooting, and their friendship.

Rarely was there a dry eye to be found, even among the "tough kids" in the crowd.

"I feel bad," Warren says, "about what I put Officer Lansford and other officers through over the years. Officer Lansford saved my life when he shot me that day. I feel better off now without my legs than when I had them."

Warren looks off in the distance for a moment. "You know," he says. "When I was little, my grandfather raised me to be a Christian, but I closed that door. Jesus didn't forget me, though."

***

This story was taken in part from an article I wrote in 1998 for *Catholic Digest*. I met with Lansford and Warren (not their real names) at a restaurant where I interviewed them at length. The atmosphere was a tad strained—no wonder: two cops and a former bad guy—but we were all polite and respectful of each other's journey. They showed me a picture of the gun's open cylinder and the four dented primers. I have lost contact with both men, and I hope they are doing well.

DIVINE INTERVENTION IN THE NEWS

Utah

A Utah woman was driving home at 10 p.m. with her 18-month-old daughter beside her in a car seat. For some unknown reason, the mother lost control. The car went off the road into the Spanish Fork River, killing her, and leaving the toddler hanging upside down in her car seat just above the freezing water.

The child would remain upside down for the next 13 hours.

The next day, a fisherman called the police and said he had spotted the overturned car. Three police officers and four firefighters arrived at the scene, and all waded into the freezing water. It was so cold the seven men were subsequently transported to the hospital and treated for hypothermia.

What happened during the rescue has left the men and everyone that hears about it baffled.

"The only people in the [submerged car] were the deceased mother and the child," one officer said. "We were down in the water, and we heard a distinct voice say, 'Help me, help me.'"

Another officer adamantly said, "It wasn't just something in our heads. And it wasn't the child. To me, it was as plain as day."

One of the officers even answered the voice. "We're trying. We're trying our best to get you out of there."

Another officer added, "We've gotten together to talk about it, and all four of us can swear we heard somebody inside the car, saying 'Help.' But we're not sure where the voice came from."

The baby survived.

Source: *All News Pipeline*

*

Oklahoma

Two officers were patrolling an unfamiliar road in the country, tree-lined on one side and pastures on the other.

"A lot of what we do is just police instinct," one of the officers told the news cameras. "And the other is just blind luck. But what happened last night had nothing to do with either. It was … divine intervention."

The officers were patrolling when something caught the driver's eye off to his right. It was a gravel road, practically hidden in the weeds. They slowed, and that's when they saw the tail light on an old truck 30 feet off the road in the tall grass. Thirty minutes later it would have been dark and impossible to see.

The officers approached the truck and instantly knew something was wrong with how the man was acting. When the driver shifted into reverse, they thought for a moment he was going to try to ram them. But when he hesitated, the officers quickly made their approach.

"At first we didn't see the little two-year-old girl in the truck. But we could see that the man's pants were undone. I asked him what was going on."

Then they saw the child.

One officer grabbed the man, and the other grabbed the little girl.

That's when the call came over the police radio that the child was missing. Her physical description and her clothing matched perfectly the child they had just saved.

The twice-convicted sex offender is now behind bars.

Source: *News on 6*

*

North Carolina

The lieutenant had gotten off duty three hours earlier when he saw a car run a stop sign.

"I heard the Lord speak to me," he said. "Get the car stopped."

Though most police officers know it's not a good idea to get involved with minor traffic infractions when they are off duty, the lieutenant went after the car. Within seconds a high-speed chase reached 115 mph.

When the car finally pulled over to the side of the road, the driver bolted into the woods. The lieutenant started to pursue but stopped when he heard screaming coming from the trunk.

"I would have run him down," the lieutenant said. "But when you hear screaming coming from a trunk that takes priority."

He managed to enter the trunk and freed a woman who had been kidnapped.

She told officers she had stopped for gas when a pregnant woman asked for a ride. When the driver agreed, the woman's boyfriend also jumped into the car.

The couple said they had a gun, and ordered her to drive them to another location where they robbed her of her cell phone and cash. They then forced her into the trunk. The man drove, dropped off his pregnant partner somewhere, and then continued with the kidnapped woman still trapped in the back.

Officers later arrested the couple.

"We don't' know what their purpose was going to be," a police spokesperson said. "I'm just glad we were able to intervene."

The woman now refers to the officer had her guardian angel.

Source: *The Blaze*

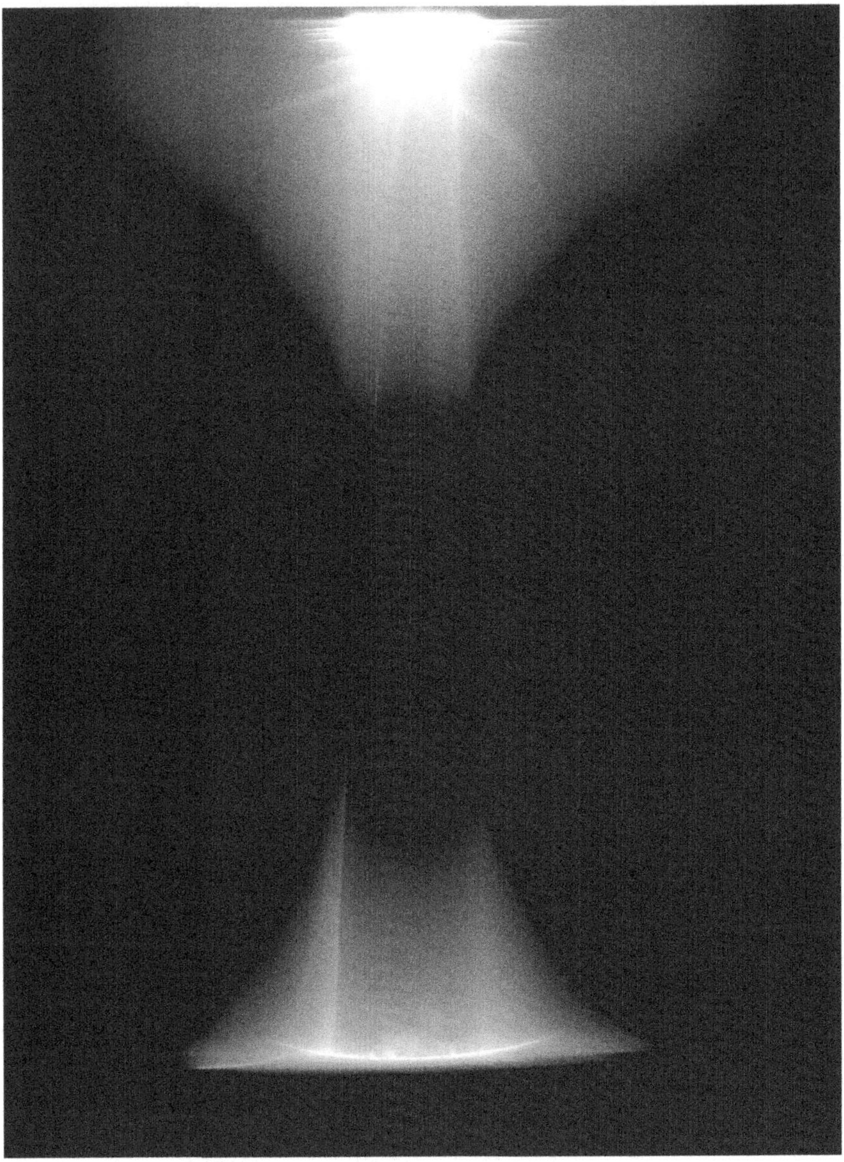

SECTION FOUR

UFOS

I was in the fourth grade when news about UFOs seemed to be everywhere. I would clip the newspaper stories and read them to my class. Some kids laughed at them while others were frightened. Little did I know that in a dozen years I would experience UFOs up close and personal, and I'd be ordered by the military brass not to tell anyone, including family and friends.

The acronym UFO was coined by the United States Air Force in 1953, about three years before I read the stories to Mrs. Clark's class. UFO stands for an unidentified flying object, meaning the thing seen is unknown. Still, most people associate it with a spacecraft from another world.

When researching early news stories, I came across the January 25, 1878 edition of the *Denison Daily News*, which contained an article about a Texas farmer who saw a large, dark, circular object flying over his property. At least the doubters couldn't argue that it was a secret government airplane or, more ominously, a Russian spy plane, since the Wright brothers were still nearly three decades away from developing their first flying machine.

There are reports of UFO sightings somewhere in the world every day. Are all of them valid? No. After we exclude hoaxers, attention seekers, and witnesses who are just plain goofy, the remaining are possibly credible. Of these—regardless of the witnesses solid standing in the community and their believability—are people susceptible to error. For example, what they saw and believed to be a UFO was really a bright planet, moon, legitimate aircraft, clouds, falling stars, or an eye floater.

Once all those things have been removed from the equation, what remains are sightings of unidentified flying objects, UFOs.

Skeptics argue that the only reason unidentified sightings cannot be explained by conventional means is because all the evidence has yet to be gathered. They contend that a sighting that remains unexplained doesn't automatically mean the object was part of an alien invasion. Similarly, the fact it cannot be proven that aliens didn't abduct a woman shouldn't, therefore, default to the belief that she was. And just because pilots, astronauts, and scientists cannot explain a given sighting, it doesn't automatically mean aliens are here.

Or, if I may, all these things just might mean they are related to alien visitation.

Skeptics would argue that because the UFOs in my story that follows were not identified doesn't automatically mean they were from Mars. True. But how would I know they weren't identified as coming from somewhere beyond Earth? I was a lowly army specialist with all the status of an earthworm. I didn't have an inside to the bigwigs at Homestead Air Force Base. I wouldn't know what occurred after the colonel and his associates visited my missile battery and ordered us not to shoot at the objects and not to tell anyone.

All I know for sure is what we saw, what the radar picked up, and how the flying craft affected our dogs, the zillions of insects and animals in the surrounding jungle, and experienced military policemen and missile specialists.

CLOSE ENCOUNTERS OF THE SECOND KIND
By Loren W. Christensen

Nocturnal Lights: Lights in the sky at night.

Radar Visual: UFO reports that have radar confirmation.

Close Encounters of the First Kind: Visual sightings of an unidentified flying object less than 500 feet away that show an appreciable angular extension and considerable detail.

Close Encounters of the Second Kind: A UFO event in which a physical effect is alleged. This can be interference in the functioning of a vehicle or electronic device; a reaction in animals; a physiological effect, such as paralysis, heat, and discomfort in the witness; or some physical trace: impressions in the ground, scorched or otherwise affected vegetation, or a chemical trace.

Close Encounters of the Third Kind: UFO encounters in which an animated creature is present. These include humanoids, robots, and humans who seem to be occupants or pilots of a UFO.

~ Based on the Hynek Classification.

Before I went to Vietnam, I was stationed in the Florida Keys working as an Army Military Police Dog Handler on a missile battery, one of four in the area, each with missiles aimed at Cuba. The bases were built earlier in the decade during the Cuban Crisis, that scary period that brought us to the brink of World War III.

To find mine, you had to enter Key Largo from the mainland, hang a tight left turn onto a winding, one-lane road, and continue for seven miles through an encroaching, claustrophobic jungle that bumped into the Everglades. There you would find a fenced military base—B company headquarters—set on a 50-acre clearing. It was smallish by military standards, with an L-shaped building that housed offices, a barracks for 60 men, a small chow hall, and radar dishes. The three large missile barns, each containing six missiles, were set in another cleared-out area of the jungle about a mile down the road.

While both locations were well-groomed with cemented walkways, asphalt roadways, high cyclone fences, and an assortment of buildings, the cutback jungle, teaming with creepy life forms of every size and shape, hunkered patiently to reclaim what it had owned for eons.

I was one of several MP dog handlers. We slept and ate in the living quarters during the day, and at night we patrolled with our dogs between two fences around the missile barns. The barriers were about eight-foot-high with a 6-foot expanse of grass between them to allow the dog handlers to patrol with German Shepherds. Throughout the acreage, Army engineers had brought in tons of gravel to make long, 25-foot-high berms. Should one of the missiles have accidentally blown, the massive hills would have forced the blast upward. While we would have been part of the mushroom cloud, it would have protected the good people of Key Largo. At least that was what the town was told. The missile guys knew it was a lie concocted to stop the citizens from complaining about the catastrophic arsenal in their backyard.

Almost every night we would climb to the top of the berms with our K9s and listen to a transistor radio station that played mellow midnight jazz, and gaze east over a half-mile of jungle to the ocean, or west over a tangled panorama that went on forever.

It was on one of those nights that we first saw the nocturnal lights.

Nocturnal Lights

There were three of them out over the ocean to the east. Brighter and larger than Venus, they moved about in no specific pattern. They would float or fly lethargically far from one another while at other times they appeared to nearly collide. There was no way to accurately determine how far or close they were to each other because we didn't know how far away they were from us.

At first, we wondered if they could have been from Homestead Air Force Base, 35 miles away on the mainland. But what kind of aircraft could maneuver and hang in the sky like that? We watched them for several hours until we had to leave for a short while. When we returned, they were gone.

But they were back the next night, and they had brought two others with them, all moving about randomly in the general vicinity they had the night before.

From our position high on the berm, we could see east over the half-mile of jungle—just a black mass at night—but not the ocean. We tried again to estimate how far the lights were from the battery and how high in the sky, but it was impossible to do so with accuracy. That said, I speculated three to five miles away and only a few hundred feet above the water.

The sightings continued for about two weeks, two or three nights a week. Sometimes there was just one light, other times as many as six. We told our command about it, but we never heard anything back.

Next to the line of kennels was the "dog shack," a small building in which we kept K-9 gear, 50-pound bags of food, and cleaning tools. There was also a sink and a counter long enough for a guy to stretch out on for a quick snooze in the wee hours of the morn. Above it, a small window.

I was sleeping on it one night when something woke me. I lay there for a few minutes looking out at the cotton ball clouds that dotted the dark sky. There was a mile of jungle between where I was sprawled and where everyone except us dog handlers was sleeping soundly in nice beds in the headquarters' building. The counter was uncomfortable, but I was enjoying a peaceful moment—until I was suddenly yanked from my serenity.

One of the cotton ball-like clouds suddenly illuminated in a neon-white light, not all of it, just around its edge. I had been stationed on the periphery of the Florida Everglades for almost a year, and I had witnessed spectacular wind and electrical storms, but I had never seen the edges of a cloud light up.

As I quickly pushed myself up to see it better, a beam of light from behind or within the cloud shot down to roughly where our headquarters was a mile down the road.

I half sprang, half fell off the counter, and ran out the door. The light beam was gone by then, though the edge of the cloud remained lit for another moment before going dark. I didn't hear a sound, and I didn't see anything fly away. I reported it, but once again I didn't hear anything back.

At least they didn't lock me up.

Years later, I saw Steven Spielberg's *Close Encounters of the Third Kind*. In the scene where Richard Dreyfuss's pickup is stalled at a railroad crossing and a beam of light from above floods the interior of his truck, I literally sprang out of my theater seat, shouting at my buddy, "That's it! That's what I saw in Florida!"

Everyone in the battery was talking about the sky show. Some were making nervous jokes, some, like me, were taking it seriously, and others weren't saying anything. The command staff remained quiet.

One night another MP and I were walking our dogs within the double fences on the far side of the missile barns. On one side of us were the fenced-in barns and on the other a swamp from which we would occasionally hear the snap of crocodile jaws. It was pitch dark except for a few light bulbs that lit the sides of the missile barns 200 yards away. My partner and I were talking when something made us look up.

Lights, two of them, and they were straight overhead and flittering about the sky. This time it scared us.

It's one thing seeing lights moving around at a distance, but it's a game changer to see them over your head. How high? There was no way of knowing because we didn't know how large or small they were. Again, if I had to guess, I would say they were as high as a low-flying private plane.

Our dogs didn't react, though the two of us were disconcerted and wondering what we should do. We had reported the lights before, but as far as we knew it had fallen on deaf ears, or so we assumed.

I decided to call it in on a field phone attached to the fence. I had never used it before, but I figured an attack by alien invaders was as good a time as ever.

"We got two lights straight overhead," I told the duty officer, trying to sound calm and professional.

"Describe them." He listened, then, "I'm calling Homestead Air

Force Base. Stay by the phone." Five minutes later, the fence phone buzzed. "They're going up," he said, and hung up before I could ask what he meant.

I had barely cradled the phone when my partner pointed up at the dark sky in the direction of the mainland. "Jets," he said simply.

There were two of them, and they were streaking our way.

In my 23-year-old mind, I thought, "This is going to be so cool," though I was shaking in my Army boots. The aircraft passed overhead, their deafening, earth-trembling roar close behind, no doubt spooking all the critters in the swamp and jungle.

A heartbeat after they had passed, the lights were no longer there, or anywhere. Did they ascend straight up and disappear or simply vanish in thin air like a celestial magic act? It was a clear night, and we could have easily seen them if they had headed off in any of the four directions.

But they didn't—at least not observable by the naked eye.

Radar Visual

There were four missile batteries in the Everglades, and each one was "hot" one week out of the month while the other three were "cold." When we were cold, only the dog handlers were in the missile area at night; when we were hot, the place was populated with about 50 men working in the barns and manning the radar trailers.

On one of our hot nights, word went out that the radar trailer had picked up a UFO. This isn't uncommon because sometimes the identity of an aircraft on the screen isn't immediately known, hence, unidentified. Although the trailer was small and crowded with missile technicians, I pushed my way to the front of the gathering crowd. The other MPs and I had been watching the strange lights for a few weeks, and my gut was telling me that what they were seeing on the screen was related. I didn't know anything about radar, but I had seen enough movies to know that the dot was the thing of interest. But was it normal that it moved so far across the screen on each consecutive blip?

"How fast you figure it's going?" someone asked.

The technician twisted in his seat, his face pale and his eyes large, "'About fifteen hundred miles per hour."

I don't remember if what happened next occurred the same night the radar picked up the UFO or if it was a different night that same week we were hot. Either way, the event is forever burned into my memory.

Close Encounters of the Second Kind

We usually kept the dogs in their kennels when the battery was hot and the missile men were busy hurrying back and forth between the barns, radar trailers, and to what we called "the duty shack," a ranch-style house in which there were bunks, kitchen, TV, and pool tables. The eight kennels were about 100 yards away from the activity, but the clamor agitated the dogs into barking nonstop in their solo 15-foot long runs. Around midnight, the missile guys would sleep in their bunks in the barns and in the duty shack, and we would get the dogs out to patrol the quiet perimeter.

It was early evening on the night it happened, and the other MPs and I were in the duty shack eating and chatting with some of the missile guys. A wide-eyed young man burst in and shouted that one of the lights was heading toward us. We all scrambled out the doors to join a dozen others standing about and looking up at the sky over the missile barns to the west.

The lone light looked like the earlier sightings, but it was getting larger as it crept ever so slowly in its descent toward us. As first, everyone was talking excitedly back and forth and calling out to new arrivals to look up. But as the object continued to come closer, everyone quieted.

I was frightened—but trying not to let on—wondering if the duty officer, a warrant officer I had never seen before, had contacted Homestead Air Force Base.

The object was about 300 hundred yards away now and on a direct course toward the far end of the barns, descending lower and lower at a crawl-like speed.

I couldn't hear it. In fact, I didn't hear anything—not the men, dogs, jungle, or the object. All was weirdly quiet until someone shouted something and another voice did the same. My eyes were glued to the object, but I was aware of shouting men running this way and that way.

I only remember the words of one man, one hysterical man. "Raise the missiles! Get to the barns and raise the missiles!"

In his excitement, he had forgotten our missiles were ground-to-ground only.

Then all was silent again, as the object—triangular shaped with two or three multicolored lights on each of the three sides—slowly passed over our heads, close enough that we could hear a low hum.

I knew of at least one report written later that said the object was believed to be 50 feet above the ground; my estimate was 200 feet. Quite a discrepancy, but as I would learn later in civilian police work, witnesses are rarely consistent.

Could it be a plane, I wondered? But it was triangular and moving so slowly, and I had never seen lighting like that on an aircraft. At such a low altitude, somewhere between 50 and 200 feet, the engine roar should have been deafening. But its sound was only a hum: *mmmmmmmmm*. The object moved on toward the jungle between the ocean and us. Then it was gone.

Someone behind me began shouting—hysterical, incoherent. It was the warrant officer over by the duty shack. He had drawn his sidearm and people were trying to calm him. When that didn't work, they commenced wrestling with him to control his gun arm. The man had completely flipped out, but the others eventually prevailed and forced him into the duty shack.

We all looked at each other, unsure of what we were supposed to do. It was then that I noticed that the jungle was utterly quiet.

For the 10 months that I had been stationed in the Everglades, the jungle was always—*always*—alive with a cacophony of racket, big critters and a massive riot of every creepy crawly insect known and unknown to entomologists. But right then, every one of them was mute.

Including our dogs.

They should have been madly barking and howling, but they too were eerily silent. The other MPs and I hurried over to the kennels to check on them. What we found we had never before seen.

The dogs had defecated all over each of their individual cement runs; it wasn't a poop pile in a corner, as was their usual. They had erupted diarrhea-like all about, as if panicked and trying to escape the confines of their pens. My dog was in his house, cowering against the back walls. I had never seen Fritz in it because he had always sensed me coming and would greet me with great excitement; likewise, with the other handlers and their dogs. I had to coach mine out, and when he finally came, he scrunched down as if to make himself small and pressed against me.

The jungle noises returned in a few minutes, and after a lot of tender loving care, the dogs were again normal, but lethargic for a while longer. I don't remember the rest of the night, but the next morning when we were driven up to the living quarters, we were met with a surprise.

"Don't Shoot at Them."

Morning formations were rare at the battery, and when they were held, MPs didn't attend because we were still working. But as we climbed out of the van that carried us back to the company area in the morning, we were told to change into clean, pressed fatigues and be in formation at 0900 hours.

It had to be about what had taken place the night before.

Everyone except for a handful of missile men still down in the barns formed up at 0900 sharp. A moment later, our captain came out through the doors followed by Air Force brass, a lieutenant, captain, colonel, and a high-ranking sergeant, all wearing dress blues. After the colonel somberly told us to stand at ease, he began talking about the events of the night before. I won't pretend to remember what all he discussed, but I do recall two specific orders.

We were not to shoot at the objects since no one knew what they were and what capabilities they possessed.

We were not to call or write home to tell friends and family what we had been seeing, especially about what had happened the night before. He told us to go about our duties as usual and report sightings as they occur.

There was no mention of the warrant officer that was last seen being whisked away in a van, never to return. He might have been transferred elsewhere, but I always had a suspicion he was wearing a straightjacket in a mental institution.

Defying orders, I waited until no one was around the pay phone in the hallway, and then I called my parents. These events had been a momentous occasion up to that point in my life, and I felt a need to touch home. My mother was frightened for me.

There were only two or three sighting after that—lights darting about over the ocean—the same kind we saw weeks earlier from atop the gravel berm. About six weeks after that infamous night, I was transferred to Arlington, Virginia to study Vietnamese at the Defense Language Institute. After that, I was sent over to Vietnam.

Two or three months after I left Florida I read a story in the newspaper about sunbathers in Miami Beach startled by strange noises in a bright blue sky. I never saw a follow-up article.

There have been lots of sightings in Florida over the years, and they continue to the present. I found only one notation online regarding a sighting in the Everglades in 1969, the same year I was there. Some "experts" say the swamp conditions offer a perfect hiding place for UFOs to submerge and lay low, or whatever they do.

I only know what we experienced.

UFOS AND COW MUTILATIONS IN THE NEWS
By Loren W. Christensen

"What is it with cows and UFOs?" ~ my daughter

Stories of cow and other farm animal mutilation have been around for many years. UFO investigators most often point toward aliens. In some cases, evidence indicates the animals were dropped from a great height. In others, investigators found burnt grass around the carcass and residual chemicals in the soil. In one story noted here, tests of the ground around an animal showed altered nutrients.

I would think it would be difficult for pranksters to do all that.

Fingers are often pointed at Satanists as the culprits, but followers of the religion are quick to point out that it isn't their M.O. Besides, footprints and tire marks are never found near the mutilations, and how would a Satanist do all that cutting and removing of things without spilling a drop of blood? And what about the impressions in the ground indicating the animals were dropped from the sky?

Then there are the believers in silent black government helicopters hovering over farmlands, stealing animals, and returning them mutilated. The question must be asked: Why would they do that? Doesn't the government have enough money to buy a cow to study its udder and anus, two organs often found missing? Why would they return them to the pasture at the risk of being seen, when they could toss them into an incinerator on the base? And why hasn't one person from the government come forth and cry out in relief to finally get it off his chest, "I did that to those bovines! Okay? I did it!"

Having worked in the government—three years in the Army and twenty-five on a police department—I can say with confidence that two people can't keep a secret, let alone a dozen, or several dozens, like so many government conspiracy theorists claim. Case in point, in the above piece "Close Encounters of the Second Kind," I said military brass told us not to write or call home about the frightening incident we experienced. But as soon as the colonel and captain drove off, we were all doing exactly that.

Here are a few news stories about UFO sightings and cattle mutilation.

*

Montana

A married couple was driving out onto their ranch at oh-dark-30 when they came across what had been a healthy young cow lying dead in a field. When the Petersons got out to examine it closer, they discovered the animal's udder, genitals, rectum, and part of its face had been removed with stunning precision. Additionally, the missing face exposed bones as clean and white as if they had been boiled.

The Pondera County Sheriff's Office was left virtually without clues.

The rancher had found a similarly mutilated cow five years earlier on a neighbor's ranch. These weren't the first mutilations of this type, in fact, the state has experienced many of them dating back to the mid-1970s. A federal investigation was made at that time with the conclusion that natural predators killed the animals.

Peterson, who has worked a ranch all his life doesn't agree because he knows what a predator kill looks like. He told the local newspaper there was no way a bear, coyote, or wolf did it.

Even stranger is that typical predators that spend their day hunting for food leave the mutilated carcasses alone. In Peterson's recent find, birds stayed away for nearly a month before moving in to eat what was left of the cow. There is no explanation as to why they waited.

Another commonality is the lack of blood, i.e., blood pools or even splatters, the absence of footprints around the body, and circular cuts made with surgical precision.

In the 2006 case, Sheriff Kuka discovered something even more perplexing. A few feet away from the cleanly parted out cow was an impression—the same size and shape as the animal lying a few feet away. But there were no drag marks, hoof, or human footprints in the soft dirt.

It was as if the cow had fallen from the sky ... and bounced.

The sheriff checked with neighbors, and no one heard low flying aircraft.

Sources: *Great Falls Tribune*

*

Missouri

A Northland farmer near Kansas City Missouri called the police to report the mutilation of a cow. Officers found the animal and discovered that its sex organs and udder had been removed.

The cow had been ill for a while and had been relocated to a pasture away from the rest of the herd. The farmer told police it had been on the mend when he checked on it the night prior.

The farmer initially thought the suspect had to have been a veterinarian, given the precision of the organ removal. But that proved not to be the case. One vet did say that the removal of parts was amazing because there should have been mass bleeding. But there wasn't.

Officers said the gate was still locked and there were no footprints or tire marks in the area.

A friend of the victim rancher said the same thing happened to one of his cows 30 years earlier.

When the vet was asked for an explanation, he leaned back a little and looked up at the sly.

Source: *Fox4 TV*

*

Missouri

Someone or something cut out the tongues and reproductive organs of numerous cows in Henry County, Missouri. Sheriff Deputy Robert Hills says they first discovered a mutilated cow in the winter of 2011 and the next two in July of 2013. All three were female and owned by the same rancher.

"We couldn't see any signs of trauma," the deputy said. "It doesn't appear there were any types of wild animal involved, such as coyotes."

There was, however, a charred outline in the grass around the latest cow mutilation.

The two mutilated in 2013, died 10 days apart. Both had their tongues, udders, anus, ears, and reproductive organs removed. For whatever reason, a veterinarian wasn't called to investigate the first two incidences, but one was asked to examine the third mutilated cow.

"The cuts were precise and surgical," the vet told the deputy. He said the cows had not been shot.

As is often the case in farm animal mutilation, there was no blood found or other bodily fluids in the immediate vicinity or in the animal. This was despite the fact some of the wounds were gaping.

The rancher later contacted Mutual UFO Network (MUFON) and told them the third cow's heart had been removed but not taken.

With no other reasonable explanation available, and given the remoteness of her ranch in the countryside, the rancher wonders if that leaves the possibility of alien involvement. "Something happened to these cows," she said. As with other farmers and ranchers, animal death was not unusual to her, whether it's natural causes or the result of attacks by wild animals.

But this situation was not in her norm.

Other cases of animal mutilation have been reported in the state over the past few years. [See the above news story]

Sources: *CBS St. Louis, KMOX, 41 Action News*

*

Pennsylvania

A woman in Paxton Township, Pennsylvania was relaxing on her front porch when she noticed a large circle of flashing lights over her home in the dark summer skies. She had never seen anything like it before, let alone above her home. She grabbed a cell phone and shot a video of it before calling her neighbor over who also witnessed the anomaly.

She told *ABC News* that she thought it was an airplane until she realized it wasn't moving. "I watched it for about 20 minutes," she said, "and then it started changing colors." Her neighbor thought it was a planet until it abruptly turned yellow. That's when she called the police.

A Paxton Township officer arrived, and he too didn't know what the lights were. After he called two other officers to verify what he was seeing, they notified a nearby airport as well as the National Guard.

Neither had flights in the area.

This occurred on a Monday night. Tuesday they didn't see anything unusual but Wednesday the lights returned.

Lt. Gary Seefeldt told the media that his "officers saw something that was out of the ordinary for the night sky."

I emailed Lt. Seefeldt and asked about the story. He concurred that his officers did respond and did see the lights. When I asked to talk to the responding officers, he said he would get a hold of them. He didn't get back to me.

Before he stopped emailing, he told me that a couple of days after the sightings, a local farmer reported that some of his cows were missing from his pasture.

Were the incidences related? He didn't know.

Sources:
New York Daily News, ABC News, Good Morning America

*

Kansas

Harvey County Sheriff's office responded to a call regarding a mutilated cow worth $5000 found in a pasture about a quarter mile off a nearby road. Its sex organs had been removed.

Initially, the farmer and the sheriff's office thought the cow had been shot before the genitals were taken. A veterinarian conducted an autopsy and said the animal had not been shot.

The vet didn't find a cause of death, and the sheriff's office couldn't find a motive for the killing.

Source: *KWCH TV*

*

Colorado

"You don't see any predator markings at all—bite marks, claw marks—and if you did it would be a clear giveaway," said Chuck Zukowski, a former volunteer sheriff's deputy in Pueblo, Colorado.

Beginning in 1999, rancher Tom Miller has lost several cows and calves to mutilation. Early on, he thought the missing ears, organs, and eyes were the product of a cruel joke. But then he began to think differently. How could pranksters remove body parts and remove sections of hide without leaving tracks or blood?

Zukowski also investigates UFO sightings and has studied 24 similar cases in Trinidad and Southern Colorado. He said the area around the cow was completely devoid of blood. He asks rhetorically how and why an animal, or any type of scavenger, would cut a round circle on one side of a cow's head? Not only that, how could an animal do it and not make a bloody mess? If a human did it, he asks, where are the footprints and tire marks?

"In other cases that I investigate," he said, "there's no sign the animal struggled. In some cases, it looks like the animal was dropped there." In a tree above one cow, he found broken branches, as if the animal had been dropped and crashed through them.

On one occasion, he found high radiation readings around the animal and, in another, changed soil nutrients.

Source: *The Pueblo Chieftain*

*

Colorado

Two police agencies investigated reports of objects seemingly floating and moving about in the sky.

Witnesses said the three objects would sometimes form a triangle and then move into a straight line.

Even the media weighed in and said the objects were not drones or balloons because they would remain motionless for as long as 15 minutes in their camera-view screens.

Many people witnessed them and called the police who called the FAA. NORAD, North American Aerospace Defense Command said they were investigating, as well.

Source: *13 WMAZ News*

CONCLUSION

Paranormal experiences are those beyond our normal grasp of the way things are supposed to be. They are even beyond scientific explanation. Paranormal events happen every day and every night to people from every walk of life around the globe. They are usually mysterious, strange, and sometimes frightening to those who witness them.

As I said in the beginning, many law enforcement officers see and experience in a month more than some people see and experience in a lifetime. It's the nature of the job: They go toward trouble while others flee from it. As a result, they are assailed with violence, horror, grief, loss, rage, and a host of other sights, sounds, and emotions. They have seen it all, and few things surprise them anymore.

But on one call, perhaps more than one, they experienced something they have never seen, heard, or felt before, on the job or off. It doesn't fit. It doesn't compute.

There is no explanation except for one.

I have always had an interest in ghosts, spirits, UFOs, ESP, and so on. But when I first thought of the idea of compiling stories from law enforcement on the subject, I was convinced I would be mocked and ran out of town. But just the opposite happened. The first day I announced the project on a Facebook law enforcement site, I got an overwhelmingly positive response. In fact, I got a story sent to me the first day. Then in the days that followed, I received more and more.

A few officers said that by writing their story, and then seeing it after I edited and formatted it for the book, they were finally able to come to a place in their mind where they felt better about their experience. What did they feel or think before? I have no idea, and I didn't intrude by asking. I certainly felt better after telling my experiences.

I know three of the officers who contributed pieces to this book. The others I got to know just a little while working on their stories with them. All are highly professional—some are past and present military, SWAT officers, and command personnel—and all wanted their stories told.

I hope you enjoyed them.

"Unpleasant dreams!" ~ Elvira, Mistress of the Dark

Are you in law enforcement and have a paranormal story you want to tell? Please contact me through my website: www.lwcbooks.com

ABOUT THE AUTHOR

Loren W. Christensen has been involved in law enforcement since 1967. He began as a 21-year-old military policeman in the US Army, serving stateside and as patrolman in Saigon, Vietnam during the war, which at that time was said to be the most dangerous city in the world. At 26, he joined the Portland, Oregon Police Bureau working a variety of jobs to include street patrol, gang enforcement, intelligence, bodyguarding, and academy trainer, retiring after 25 years. He has trained various security agencies in arrest and control tactics, and officer survival.

The very next day after leaving the PD, Loren began a full-time career as a writer, now with nearly 60 books in print with five publishers, as well as magazine articles, and blog pieces. He edited a police newspaper for nearly seven years. His nonfiction includes books on the martial arts, police work, PTSD, mental preparation for violence, meditation, nutrition, exercise, and various subcultures, to include prostitution, street gangs, skid row, and riots.

His fiction series *Dukkha* was a finalist in the prestigious USA Best Book Awards.

Loren's books have been translated into five languages.

As a martial arts student and teacher since 1965, Loren has earned a total of 11 black belts in three arts and was inducted into the Masters Hall of Fame in 2011.

OTHER BOOKS BY LOREN W. CHRISTENSEN

The following are available on Amazon, from their publishers, and through the usual book outlets. Signed copies can be purchased at LWC Books, www.lwcbooks.com

Nonfiction

Street Stoppers
Fighting In The Clinch
Fighter's Fact Book
Fighter's Fact Book 2
Solo Training
Solo Training 2
Solo Training 3
Speed Training
The Fighter's Body
Total Defense
The Mental Edge
The Way Alone
Far Beyond Defensive Tactics
Fighting Power
Crouching Tiger
Anything Goes
Winning With American Kata
Total Defense
Riot
Warriors
On Combat
Warrior Mindset
Deadly Force Encounters
Surviving Workplace Violence
Surviving A School Shooting
Gangbangers
Skinhead Street Gangs
Hookers, Tricks And Cops

Way Of The Warrior
Skid Row Beat
Defensive Tactics
Missing Children
Fight Back: Self-Defense For Women
Extreme Joint Locking
Timing In The Martial Arts
Fighter's Guide to Hard-Core Heavy Bag Training
The Brutal Art Of Ripping, Poking And Pressing Vital Targets
How To Live Safely In A Dangerous World
Fighting The Pain Resistant Attacker
Evolution Of Weaponry
Meditation For Warriors
Mental Rehearsal For Warriors
Prostate Cancer
Musings On Violence
Policing Saigon
Cops' True Stories Of The Paranormal

Fiction

Novels:
Dukkha: The Suffering
Dukkha: Reverb
Dukkha: Unloaded
Dukkha: Hungry Ghosts

Short Stories:

Old Ed
Old Ed 2
Old Ed 3
Old Ed 4
Old Ed 5
Old Ed Omnibus

Boss
Boss 2
Boss 3
Boss Omnibus

Parts

DVDs

Solo Training
Fighting Dirty
Speed Training
Masters And Styles
Vital Targets
The Brutal Art of Ripping, And Pressing Vital Targets
Restraint and Control Strategies

YOU MIGHT ALSO LIKE

Inspired by actual events in
*Cops' True Stories of the Paranormal:
Ghosts, UFOs, and Other Shivers*

PARTS
A Short Story

Loren W. CHRISTENSEN
BEST-SELLING COAUTHOR OF *ON COMBAT*

Made in the USA
Coppell, TX
18 November 2019